I Used to
Know That
PHILOSOPHY

"Philosophy begins in wonder. And, at the end, when philosophic thought has done its best, the wonder remains."

—ALFRED NORTH WHITEHEAD

A Gift for

_____

Presented by

_____

I Used to Know That

PHILOSOPHY

stuff you forgot from school

LESLEY LEVENE

The Reader's Digest Association, Inc.
New York, NY / Montreal

A READER'S DIGEST BOOK

Copyright © 2011 Michael O'Mara Books Limited

All rights reserved. Unauthorized reproduction, in any manner, is prohibited.

Reader's Digest is a registered trademark of The Reader's Digest Association, Inc.

First published in Great Britain in 2010 by Michael O'Mara Books Limited,
9 Lion Yard, Tremadoc Road, London SW4 7NQ

READER'S DIGEST TRADE PUBLISHING
Consulting Editor: Susan Randol
Copy Editor: Barbara Booth
Project Production Coordinator: Rich Kershner
Senior Art Director: George McKeon
Executive Editor, Trade Publishing: Dolores York
Manufacturing Manager: Elizabeth Dinda
Associate Publisher, Trade Publishing: Rosanne McManus
President and Publisher, Trade Publishing: Harold Clarke

Library of Congress Cataloging in Publication Data
Levene, Lesley.
 Philosophy : stuff you forgot from school / Lesley Levene.
   p. cm. -- (I used to know that)
 Includes bibliographical references and index.
 ISBN 978-1-60652-323-0
 1. Philosophy--Introductions 2. Philosophy--History. I. Title.
 BD21.L44 2011
 100--dc22
                        2011010083

Reader's Digest is committed to both the quality of our products and the service
we provide to our customers. We value your comments, so please feel free to contact us: The Reader's Digest Association, Inc., Adult Trade Publishing,
44 S. Broadway, White Plains, NY 10601

For more Reader's Digest products and information, visit our website:
 www.rd.com (in the United States)
www.readersdigest.ca (in Canada)

Printed in the United States of America

1 3 5 7 9 10 8 6 4 2

I would like to thank Louise Dixon and Silvia Crompton at Michael O'Mara Books
for their patience throughout, and various friends—especially Annie Lee, Richard
Sandover and Peter Spencer—who have helped by providing advice, books and a
sympathetic ear or two. Moreover, I hereby swear that, in my other life as an
editor, I will never again moan about authors who deliver their books late.

For Jose and Cyril Levene and Ruth and Peter Spencer—all of whom have good reason to view life philosophically.

CONTENTS

What's It All About, Then?

> "All are lunatics, but he who can analyze his delusion
> is called a philosopher."
> —Ambrose Bierce, *Epigrams*

The very fact that this book ranges over some two and a half thousand years suggests the answer: that there is no answer. What is clear, however, is that people have been asking philosophical questions in an effort to understand the world and their role in it for as long as records have existed.

In the introduction to his *History of Western Philosophy*, Bertrand Russell points out that philosophy straddles the fields of science and theology, attempting to apply human reason to speculations in areas where definite knowledge is not yet available. The fascinating thing is that as more knowledge becomes available, the questions still remain. Which is fine, because there's nothing like a bit of healthy speculation—as long as you are well informed.

By looking at the development of philosophical ideas over time, placing individual philosophers against their historical and social backgrounds to get a sense of what was influencing their thinking, this book aims to provide you with the wherewithal to speculate with the best of them.

9

THE PRESOCRATIC PHILOSOPHERS

The name says it all: the Presocratics were around before Socrates. A number of early thinkers from the ancient world, some of whom might even have known of his ideas, can be grouped together under this heading. Dating from the late seventh century to the fifth century B.C., they all attempted in their different ways to explain how the world was constituted and to explore the nature of reality. In other words, they were trying to answer the great "What's it all about, then?" question.

The earliest Presocratic philosophers came from Ionia, midway along the west coast of Asia Minor. The area, which is now part of Turkey, had been colonized by the Greeks from about 1000 B.C. and, by the time our Presocratics came along, was home to a number of flourishing city-states. These prospered as a result of trade and cultural links with Egypt and Babylonia (present-day Iraq) to the east, both renowned for their ancient wisdom, as well as with the Greek colonies on the Black Sea and the Greek mainland farther west. Moreover,

Ionia had a literary heritage linking it via Homer to the riches of Mycenae.

Such conditions must have fostered a vigorous intellectual life, because there certainly seems to have been much interest in speculative thought in the major centers of population—Miletus, Ephesus, Colophon and Samos—and great thinkers from here, together with their ideas, gradually began to exert an influence that spread into the world beyond.

Thales
(c. 624–c. 545 B.C.)

According to Aristotle, who presumably knew what he was talking about, Thales of Miletus was the first real philosopher, which makes him the founder not just of Greek but ultimately of European philosophy. Unfortunately, he left behind no body of work, so his opinions are known only from later reports, but he seems to have had wide-ranging practical and intellectual interests and was renowned as an engineer, a mathematician, an astronomer and a statesman. He is said to have traveled to Egypt, where he pursued his interest in trigonometry—it was presumably some sort of mathematical hot spot—and to have used Babylonian celestial charts to accurately predict a solar eclipse in 585 B.C.

What makes it possible to talk about Thales and the later Presocratics as philosophers—rather than, say, brilliant mathematicians or astronomers—is the fact that they believed the world had an underlying unity, something physical that could be pinned down, studied and understood rationally in order to identify how it had come into being. Of course, there was one small snag: they had no idea what this miraculous substance was.

There would be plenty of false starts, but the search itself signaled a move away from mythology as an explanation for events. Rather than looking to the frankly irrational behavior of the gods to answer questions about why things were as they were, these early philosophers attempted to come up with systematic accounts of the visible world in straightforward descriptive and analytical terms.

For Thales, water was the key. Having seen the way it could take on different forms (mist, ice and so on), he decided that water must be the basis of the universe—literally, in fact, since he thought that the flat earth floated on water and that earthquakes were caused when big waves hit the land.

He was cited as one of the Seven Wise Men by Plato in his *Protagoras* but was more the absent-minded professor in a number of anecdotes, such as the one that had him stumbling into a ditch because he was too busy studying the stars to watch where he was going.

Anaximander
(610–546 B.C.)

Born in Miletus, Anaximander was quite possibly a pupil of Thales. Like Thales, he had a number of scientific interests: he produced the first (admittedly wildly inaccurate) map of the world, he studied meteorology (declaring that thunder was the banging together of clouds), and he introduced the gnomon (the upright arm of the sundial) to the Greek world. A statesman, too, he was chosen as leader of his city's new Black Sea colony, Apollonia. He was also Thales's successor on the philosophical front, actually writing down his ideas—another first—although he disagreed with the premise that water, or indeed any one physical element, could be the first principle.

Anaximander argued that if water were given preeminence, other elements, such as fire, would be excluded: while water might change into mist and ice, it could not encompass the opposites wet and dry. He preferred to look for a more universal originating substance, one that was not bounded by physical characteristics. He came up with the notion of "the indefinite," *apeiron*, from which all things are created and to which all things return, and suggested that the universe and all its elements and opposites came into being only when separation from the indefinite took place.

To be more specific, Anaximander said that when heat and cold had escaped from the *apeiron*, the heavier cold mist solidified to form the Earth—a broad cylinder that sits unsupported at the center of the universe—while the heat had expanded out into huge wheels of flame circling the earth. The air between the earth and the fire creates a mist, and it is only through gaps in this mist that we can perceive chinks of light from the fiery wheels—or what we now know to be stars and planets. Within the world, pairs of linked opposites—wet/dry, hot/cold and so on—resulting from the initial separation constantly seek to return to the indefinite, providing rhythm and unity to the universe.

Anaximander also theorized that human beings—who originally had spines on their skin, like fish—had emerged from the slime left behind once the waters drew back from the land. In short, the early Presocratic obsession with water was still very much alive.

Anaximenes
(*fl. c.* 545 B.C., C. 528 B.C.)

There's a third one from Miletus, though sadly no biographical details about him exist. Anaximenes seems to have reverted to Thales's idea that there was one basic form of matter—in this case, *aer* (air or mist)—but he proposed that this single substance could be transformed into other substances according to its degree of concentration. Rarefied it became fire; condensed it formed water and earth. As well as making the obvious links with the physical world (the sun as fire in the sky, lightning emerging from clouds, mist falling as rain), Anaximenes connected air with the breath of life, the soul, thus drawing upon Anaximander's "indefinite." For Anaximenes, the earth was flat and floated on the air like a leaf, as did the heavenly bodies, fiery disks that had been formed from rarefied rising vapor.

Pythagoras
(c. 570–c. 490 B.C.)

Born on the Greek island of Samos, Pythagoras—yes, he of the theorem—is said to have visited both Egypt and Babylonia before settling at Croton, a Greek colony in southern Italy, in about 530 B.C. Here he established a community that eventually became both a mathematical school and a religious group. As he left behind no written works, most of what we know about Pythagoras comes from later accounts, many of which were obviously embellished over time, assuming the form of myths and legends. Among other things, he is described as having a golden thigh and is credited with the ability to be in two places at once, as well as to project writing from a mirror onto the moon.

On a more practical level, Pythagoras observed that musical notes differed according to the different lengths of an instrument's strings, deducing from this that mathematical ratios were what underpinned musical harmony (in the process also introducing the concept of musical intervals). From there he went on to assert that mathematics lay at the heart of reality—not water, not air, but numbers. It was numbers that defined (think of Anaximander's "indefinite") the shapes and forms of physical objects, just as they determined the movement of the stars and other celestial bodies, a harmonious mathematical relationship known as the music of the spheres.

From here, Pythagoreanism developed as much as a way of life as a philosophy. Its adherents favored a contemplative, abstemious lifestyle, living communally, with men and women treated equally and property held in common. They were seeking their own form of earthly harmony through moral asceticism and ritual purification of the body (beans were strictly off limits, as was meat) and the soul. Pythagoras held that all living things were related and believed in the transmigration of souls—in other words, that the soul was immortal and passed on to a different body after death—claiming that he had been other people in earlier lives.

Many of Pythagoras's ideas later found expression in the writings of Plato, most obviously the emphasis on a pure reality—as manifested for Pythagoras in mathematics and the immortality of the soul—underlying imperfect appearances.

> PYTHAGORAS OBSERVED THAT MUSICAL NOTES DIFFERED ACCORDING TO THE DIFFERENT LENGTHS OF AN INSTRUMENT'S STRINGS, DEDUCING FROM THIS THAT MATHEMATICAL RATIOS WERE WHAT UNDERPINNED MUSICAL HARMONY.

Xenophanes

(C. 570–C. 475 B.C.)

It was probably in 546 B.C., when the victorious armies of Cyrus the Great swept through Asia Minor, that Xenophanes left his home in Colophon. For the rest of his life, he wandered around the Mediterranean, basing himself for a time in Sicily and also visiting Elea in southern Italy, home to an important group of philosophers with whom he was later linked. He wrote poetry, fragments of which survive, and these, together with references in other people's works, give us an idea of his wide-ranging interests.

Xenophanes posed one of the knottiest and most enduring of philosophical questions: How can any of us honestly claim to know the truth about things we haven't seen for ourselves? In other words, he pointed out that there's a big difference between opinion and true knowledge and that, while truth exists, we can only speculate about it. From there he turned his attention to a whole host of topics.

On the religious front, rather than rejecting random acts by the gods as an explanation for events, he actively criticized the traditional Homeric approach of attributing our human failings—adultery, theft, deceit (so no change there)—to the gods. Xenophanes argued that this endorsed immoral behavior, along with such anthropomorphism—the giving of human characteristics to nonhumans—led to logical absurdities. It was confusing enough that Ethiopians had black-haired gods and Thracians had red-haired ones, but what about horses and cattle? How would their gods look? Instead, he suggested that there was a single supreme deity, spherical like the world, eternal and unchanging, totally different from humans in appearance and nature, who operated through the power of his mind.

Pursuing his interest in promoting moral behavior among his fellow citizens, Xenophanes also spoke out against excessive drinking, the acquisition of unnecessary luxuries and the ludicrous honors heaped on successful athletes—all of which sounds remarkably familiar. Less so, and on a more down-to-earth level, when he saw fossils of fish far from the sea, he concluded that the Earth had once been covered by water, going on to propose that earth and water in various combinations formed the basis of all things, with clouds a transitional state.

Heraclitus

(c. 535–475 B.C.)

Born in Ephesus into an established aristocratic family, Heraclitus seems to have had no interest in participating in public life, refusing favors from the Persian authorities on the grounds that he did not care for luxury. He had even less interest in making himself popular—he was forever accusing people of stupidity, going so far as to single out Xenophanes as someone who had no sense despite all his learning. He is believed to have written a book called *On Nature*, of which only fragments remain, and these, together with the responses of other writers to his work, give us some idea of his opinions.

Heraclitus is best known for his assertion that everything exists in a state of permanent flux, so it is little wonder that he gained the nickname the Obscure. As he explained it, you can never step into the same river twice for the simple reason that the water you

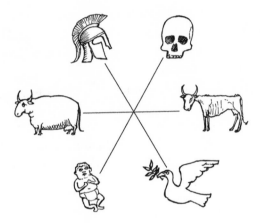

dip your toes into on the second occasion is not the same water you touched the first time around. The world might *appear* to be a stable, unified whole—which was what prompted Thales, Anaximander and others to look for a single unifying component—but Heraclitus felt that this missed the point. Rather than seeing permanence and stability, he declared that beneath the surface, the world could be understood in terms of a continuous struggle between pairs of opposites. The examples he gave ranged from the fairly pedestrian—up/down, hot/cold, wet/dry, day/night—to the downright extreme: life/death, war/peace, famine/plenty. Although each part of the pair was separate, neither could exist without the other, as both were merely extreme aspects of the same thing. These opposites shared a common structural feature, which Heraclitus called *logos* (reason), and it was this that, like a form of eternal cosmic justice, maintained some sort of balance and regulated the continuity of change.

For Heraclitus, then, the unity of the world existed in its underlying structure—the way it was arranged—rather than in any particular component. He did, however, identify fire as the original and most desirable element, and the physical manifestation of *logos*.

Parmenides
(C. 515–450 B.C.)

Born in the Greek colony of Elea, southern Italy, Parmenides is generally seen as the brains behind the Eleatic school, which emphasized the unchanging nature of reality. His early life is not well documented, but at the age of sixty-five, he apparently met the young Socrates, whose ideas—and by extension those of Plato—he certainly seems to have influenced. Parmenides was the first philosopher to use logic and language to reach conclusions about the world that didn't rely on observation, and indeed often flew directly in the face of it.

His opinions have come down to us through the surviving 150 or so lines of a much longer three-part poem called—once again—*On Nature*. In the first part he describes meeting a goddess who promises to reveal to him both "the way of truth," or reality, and "the way of seeming," or opinion; these then form the second and third parts of the poem. Basically, as far as reality goes, if we can think and talk about something, logic says it must exist—it *is*—since it makes no sense to think or talk about something that doesn't exist and which *is not*.

If you can get your head around that, explains Parmenides, it surely follows that there was nothing before (the past) and there is nothing to come (the future), as both imply nonbeing in the present, and this in turn means that there has never been

ZENO'S PARADOXES

A follower of Parmenides—he of the static, unchanging universe—Zeno of Elea (c. 490—430 B.C.) came up with a number of teasing paradoxes to demonstrate the impossibility of motion.

Zeno explained why it's impossible to cross from one side of a racecourse to the other. Before you can cover the whole distance, you need to cover half, and half again, and again—in other words, there are so many increasingly tiny journeys to make that you'll get nowhere fast.

Then there's the one with the arrow. You line up your target, you take aim, you fire.... But at any point during its flight, your arrow is occupying the whole of a tiny bit of space and is, in that instant, motionless. Given that its so-called "flight" is made up of a succession of motionless instances, the arrow is not actually moving at all.

Zeno met Socrates on a trip to Athens with Parmenides, as a result of which he featured in Plato's dialogue *Parmenides*, and was credited by Aristotle as being the first to use dialectic—a formal method of disputation in which opponents attempted to find inconsistencies and absurdities in each other's arguments. Which brings us back to those paradoxes again.

and never will be any change. So things continue in some sort of eternal, static, uniform present. There can be no motion, because that would imply a move into nothingness; there can be no material change, because that would imply the existence of a previous state. All of which leads to the conclusion that any sort of change we *think* we see must be illusory: the way of seeming rather than the way of truth.

The reasoning might seem artificial—whatever Parmenides' grip on logic, his argument relies on a mind-boggling interpretation of the verb "to be"—but the conflict between reality and illusion is real enough, and it's one that has continued to exercise philosophers ever since.

Anaxagoras
(c. 500—428 B.C.)

Originally from Clazomenae in Ionia, Anaxagoras spent thirty years in Athens, the first philosopher to bring this brand of intellectual enquiry to what was to become the center of the ancient Greek world. Here his teachings influenced, among others, the statesman Pericles and the playwright Euripides. When asked the point of being born, his answer was "to study the universe." Eventually these studies led him to assert that the sun was a huge incandescent lump of rock bigger than the Peloponnese, a pronouncement that seems to have upset the authorities, as he was prosecuted for impiety, convicted and subsequently banished.

To arrive at his own interpretation of the material world, Anaxagoras took Parmenides' assertion that things did not come into being or pass away and attempted to reconcile it with the visible evidence of change that existed everywhere. The result was his theory that the world had originally consisted of all kinds of natural particles mixed together, before *nous* (mind)—"the finest of all things and the purest," the driving force—started it spinning. In the vortex that ensued, the various particles combined and separated to create all manner of things, meaning that there would always be a small portion of everything in everything else—apart, that is, from in *nous*, which is "mixed with nothing." While each object's main constituent at any given time would define its identity, the ongoing combination and separation of spinning particles made change not only possible but also inevitable.

With his introduction of *nous* as the prime mover, Anaxagoras was providing a purely mechanistic explanation of how things operated. Later philosophers would take his ideas a stage further and begin to look for an underlying sense of purpose as well.

Empedocles
(c. 495–c. 435 b.c.)

Born in the Greek colony Acragas (modern Agrigento) in Sicily, Empedocles gained fame not only as a philosopher and poet but also as a doctor, a scientist and a statesman. Legend credits him with higher aspirations, too, for he is said to have thrown himself into the crater on Mount Etna to prove his godlike nature— unfortunately, Empedocles' last experiment ended then and there, as he was "roasted whole."

His main philosophical work is the poem called—yes, you guessed—*On Nature*, many fragments of which survive. Where

Parmenides saw a static, permanently unchanging universe and Anaxagoras a universe created from an unlimited number of substances mixed together, Empedocles held that all things were made from four basic and permanent elements, or "roots": earth, air, fire and water. Influenced by twin forces that he called Love and Strife, these would come together and pull apart to form different objects. The universe moved through a never-ending cycle: first Love dominated, then Strife (and with it our world) appeared on top for a time, then Love reasserted itself once more.

While it would be presumptuous to suggest a direct link to the work of Charles Darwin, it's certainly true that Empedocles talked about the origins of living creatures in such a way as to suggest some form of evolution. In his version of events, there was an initial period in which limbs wandered around on their own—calves with the faces of men, children with the heads of cattle, and other oddities—before more familiar territory was reached. He also came up with a theory explaining our awareness of things: particles of elements from other objects interact with our sense organs and enter through our pores, at which point they are detected by the corresponding particles in us.

In a second poem, *Purifications*, which may or may not be part of *On Nature* but certainly takes a more overtly religious line, Empedocles seems to have incorporated the ideas of Pythagoras and his followers on the transmigration of souls into his system. He describes the physical journey made by a soul in terms of an ongoing cycle: from a state of godlike innocence to a fall into mortality (as a result of shedding the blood of men and animals), followed by purification and deification once more, with Love and Strife again driving events.

Protagoras
(C. 490–420 B.C.)

Born in Abdera in northeastern Greece, Protagoras traveled regularly to Athens and other cities, pursuing his career as a teacher. It was in Athens that he met Pericles, who invited him to write the legal code for the new Athenian colony of Thurii in Italy—a pretty good vindication of his views on justice and virtue, which we'll come to shortly. Protagoras was possibly the first of a growing number of intellectuals known as sophists (from *sophos*, "wise"), who expounded on a range of philosophical and practical subjects and were held in such esteem that their students paid for the privilege of listening to them. He taught rhetoric, which was a fundamental requirement for taking part in public life in ancient Greece, and also poetry, grammar and syntax. According to Plato's *Protagoras*, he claimed he could teach virtue, too.

Protagoras is best known for his relativism and his agnosticism. With his assertion that "Man is the measure of all things, of the existence of the things that are and the nonexistence of the things that are not," he was signaling his belief that there were no fixed, objective standards—Parmenides, eat your heart out—but rather that things varied with the individual and with circumstances. So while you might feel hot on a summer's day in New York, someone used to living in the Sahara would find it rather cool. Protagoras took this approach a step further, pointing out that it was equally applicable to matters of beauty, virtue, truth and justice; essentially, it's all relative.

WITH HIS EMPHASIS ON THE IMPORTANCE OF SUBJECTIVITY IN HOW WE UNDERSTAND THE UNIVERSE, PROTAGORAS STARTED THE SHIFT AWAY FROM NATURAL PHILOSOPHY TOWARD AN INTEREST IN HUMAN VALUES.

Protagoras saw this relativism in a positive light, as a break from the constraints of existing philosophy and religion, opening the way for democratic debate. However, he was later criticized for allowing more unscrupulous people to play with words, making "the worse case appear better"—which explains today's negative connotations of "sophistry," using clever arguments without ethical constraints. Still, Protagoras himself and the so-called Older Sophists were known as men who respected the law.

With his emphasis on the importance of subjectivity in how we understand the universe, Protagoras started the shift away from natural philosophy toward an interest in human values. And it was in response to Sophists like him that Plato began his search for transcendent, eternal truths that underpinned the human experience.

THE GREEK
HEAVYWEIGHTS

Ask most people with the slightest interest in the subject to name a philosopher, and they will probably come up with one of the Big Three: Socrates, Plato and Aristotle. These are the names that have lasted through the centuries—these are the boys with the bright ideas. They mark, once and for all, the shift away from natural philosophy—all those books and poems entitled *On Nature*—toward the personal, with an emphasis on the use of reason in order to achieve wisdom and virtue, from which personal happiness (and, by extension on the wider stage, political well-being) can flow. It's presumably no coincidence that they were all based in Athens for long periods, at a time when the city was the intellectual and political center of the classical world.

Toward the end of the fourth century B.C., with the overshadowing of Athens and the other Greek city-states after the military exploits of King Philip II of Macedon and his son Alexander the Great, two new schools of philosophy, Epicureanism and Stoicism, fronted respectively by Epicurus and Zeno of Citium, came to the fore. They continued to exert influence throughout the Hellenistic period and into Roman times.

Socrates

(C. 470–399 B.C.)

"The unexamined life is not worth living."
—Quoted by Plato in his *Apology*

Born in Athens, Socrates left no written body of work, founded no school of philosophy and had no formal group of disciples, yet he is considered the first great figure of ancient philosophy. This is because he marks a clear break with earlier philosophical speculation about the origins and nature of the universe, turning instead to an analysis of ethics and the moral concepts by which human beings should live.

What little information we have about Socrates comes from three sources: the comic playwright Aristophanes, the military commander Xenophon and the great philosopher Plato, who was a student of Socrates. Each of them obviously had his own angle. Aristophanes portrays Socrates as a buffoon in his play *The Clouds*, while for Xenophon he was a soldier and a man of action. It is largely thanks to Plato that we know about Socrates' philosophical views. Plato outlines these in the form of dialogues, using this dramatic approach to convey both the method (dialectical reasoning) and the beliefs (the pursuit of moral good) of his master. It is thought that the *Apology* (the defense speech at Socrates' trial), *Crito* and *Phaedo* most accurately reflect Socrates' teachings.

The dialogues are presented as lengthy question-and-answer sessions with a range of people—politicians, students and friends—and explore widely held attitudes toward such fundamental concepts, or "virtues," as justice, courage, moderation, wisdom and piety. According to Plato, Socrates always claimed that he himself knew nothing. Rather than imposing his own views on others, he challenged people to defend the logical basis for their ideas, the theory being that this would force them to confront contradictions in their own arguments. Only then, when false logic had been stripped away by a process of elimination, would people accept their ignorance and seek universally applicable definitions for the virtues fundamental to human life, in the process revealing a deeper moral good.

For Socrates righteous living was the key. This included resisting the pursuit of fame and fortune and never, under any circumstances, returning evil for evil. The most important thing in life was to look after the moral welfare of one's soul, as this was the route to true happiness. It was a very personal philosophy: once the meaning of the virtues had been clarified and understood, one could become an objectively better person, unswayed by ties to family and friends.

Unfortunately for Socrates, his constant challenging of widely held beliefs eventually put him at odds with the state; he was brought to trial in 399 B.C., charged with introducing new gods and corrupting the youth.

At his trial Socrates was not to be deflected from his objective intellectual stance. He was given the option of paying a fine instead of facing the death sentence but turned it down; he was then offered the chance to escape from prison through bribery but rejected it. His reasoning was that no matter what the outcome, a citizen should always obey the laws of the state. And so, having lived uncompromisingly for philosophy, in the end he drank hemlock and died for it.

Plato

(427–347 B.C.)

"Philosophy begins in wonder."
—*Theaetetus*

Born in Athens into an aristocratic family, Plato seems to have been destined for a life in politics before he became a student of Socrates, about whose trial and subsequent death he later wrote. Disillusioned by these events, Plato left Athens in 399 B.C. and traveled to Greece and Egypt, southern Italy and Sicily. By around 387 B.C. he was back in Athens, however, and it is here that he established the Academy, which some have called the first university. It was a place for philosophical, mathematical and scientific study, with the aim of improving political life in Greek cities, and Plato presided over it for the rest of his life. Most of his works have come down to us in

---

THE ACADEMY AWARDS

Plato set up his school for philosophers in a grove dedicated to the hero Akademos, which explains why it came to be known as the Academy, which in turn explains why scholarly types are known as academics.

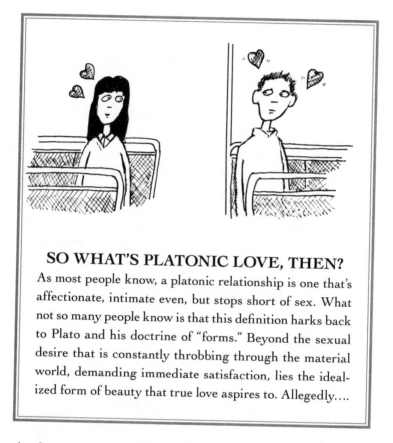

SO WHAT'S PLATONIC LOVE, THEN?

As most people know, a platonic relationship is one that's affectionate, intimate even, but stops short of sex. What not so many people know is that this definition harks back to Plato and his doctrine of "forms." Beyond the sexual desire that is constantly throbbing through the material world, demanding immediate satisfaction, lies the idealized form of beauty that true love aspires to. Allegedly....

the form of conversations, referred to as dialogues, between Socrates and a range of other people.

In the early dialogues, Socrates attempts to tease out definitions of moral virtues by grilling individuals about their beliefs: so, for example, he discusses piety with Euthyphro, an expert on religion; and courage with Laches, a general, in the dialogues that bear their names. And he goes at his task in such a rigorous, relentless way that their initially confident assertions are dismantled step by step, revealed as being riddled with inconsistencies, and everyone, Socrates included, ends up bamboozled. Which might have been a satisfying intellectual exercise for Socrates, but it no doubt drove everyone else mad.

The middle dialogues—among them *Phaedo* (a discussion of Socrates' death, which goes on to talk of immortality) and the *Republic* (considerations of justice as they relate to the individual and the state)—display a more positive, constructive approach. Here Plato outlines a number of important ideas: that the soul is immortal and consists of three parts (one that seeks to satisfy basic appetites, one that responds to active qualities such as courage, and one that is represented by the intellect); that knowledge is actually recollection of a time before our immortal soul was imprisoned in our body; and that the changing material world of objects (pale shadows we recognize only by perception, opinion or belief) masks the eternal reality of forms, which exist beyond most people's understanding. Perfect and ideal, these forms are the ultimate goal of knowledge.

The famous allegory of the cave is found in *The Republic*. Here Socrates (via Plato) describes humans as prisoners who have been chained all their life in a cave, able to perceive the world only via shadows cast on the wall in front of them by the light of a fire behind them. In other words, they see shadows rather than reality; indeed, the shadows *are* their reality. The philosopher's role in society is to leave the cave and finally see the world for what it is.

As for the soul, again, the philosopher will be able to keep all three parts in harmony, not allowing any one to dominate. And the same can be said of society, for Plato equates the three parts of the soul with the three classes of society: rulers, soldiers and the common people. For there to be a just society, each class must keep to its own sphere, with the ruler immersing himself in philosophy to aid him in his task—though when Plato twice attempted to put his theories into practice in Syracuse in the 360s B.C., instructing Dionysius II on how to become a philosopher-king, he became entangled in a political feud and was soon back in Athens.

The later dialogues backtrack on the business of forms and instead delve more deeply into concepts of knowledge, revisiting the ideal republic and exploring the natural world via physics and chemistry, physiology and medicine.

Plato's Academy continued to exist until A.D. 529, when it was closed by the Emperor Justinian in an attempt to suppress pagan Hellenistic culture, but his ideas did not disappear. Plato is still seen as the person who introduced the philosophical argument as we think of it today, while the range and depth of his interests have never been surpassed.

Aristotle

(384–322 B.C.)

"Human good turns out to be the active exercise
of the soul in conformity with excellence or virtue....
But this activity must take place throughout a complete
lifetime, for one swallow does not make a summer,
any more than one fine day."

—*Nicomachean Ethics*

The son of a doctor—in fact, *the* doctor at the court of the increasingly powerful kings of Macedon—Aristotle was born in Stagira in northern Greece. In 367 B.C. he went to Athens, where he was initially a pupil and then became a teacher at Plato's Academy. He left after twenty years, possibly miffed at not being chosen to replace Plato when the great man died, and, among other things, spent time tutoring the young Alexander (who was not yet Great). He returned to Athens in 335 B.C. and established his own school, which was called the Lyceum because it was near the site where Apollo Lycaeus, the god Apollo in a wolf incarnation, was honored. Here Aristotle taught for the next twelve years, but he had to leave on the death of Alexander (now Great) in 323 B.C., as a wave of anti-Macedonian sentiment swept through Athens, carrying him along with it.

The majority of Aristotle's work survived in the form of treatises or lecture notes. He seems to have had something to say on virtually every subject under the sun: logic, metaphysics, ethics, politics, rhetoric, poetry, literary analysis, meteorology, astronomy, biology, zoology, physics and psychology. These notes, only for serious students originally, were collected in the first century B.C. by Andronicus of Rhodes, at which point they would no doubt have been edited. This means that the first published versions of Aristotle's work, not to mention the subsequent Latin and Arabic translations, were based on someone else's interpretation, but no matter. The result is that his *Organon* (on logic), *Metaphysics*, *Nicomachean Ethics*, *Politics*, *On Rhetoric*, *Poetics* and plenty of others can still be read today.

Aristotle effectively established the science of logic, refining universal rules of reasoning to help in the pursuit of knowledge. Try this example:

step 1 All men are mortal.
step 2 Socrates is a man.
step 3 Therefore Socrates is mortal.

That's a classic bit of syllogism—that is, using deductive inference. Or, to put it more simply: if steps 1 and 2 are true, you can deduce step 3.

Then there's his work on metaphysics—the search for first principles. Everything that exists can be assigned to a category: so it's a substance or a quality or a quantity or a... (Aristotle lists as many as ten categories sometimes.) There's a hierarchy here: to stick with Socrates, the fact that he's a man (see above) means that he belongs in substance; his personal qualities cannot precede his substance. Meanwhile, substance itself is made up of matter (the physical component parts)

> ◎◎ ◎◎ ◎◎
>
> **ARISTOTLE EFFECTIVELY ESTABLISHED THE SCIENCE OF LOGIC, REFINING UNIVERSAL RULES OF REASONING TO HELP IN THE PURSUIT OF KNOWLEDGE.**
>
> ◎◎ ◎◎ ◎◎

and form (structure, which is normally determined by function). This is not "form" in Plato's sense of an idealized version that exists elsewhere, but something grounded in the here and now—the universal essence of whatever the object in question. Aristotle then identifies four causes of everything: the material cause (what something's made of); the formal cause (what it actually is); the efficient cause (its means of creation); and the final cause (its purpose).

As for ethics, Aristotle points out that, although everyone seeks the good life, "good" is not one particular quality. Before

ARE YOU A CYNIC?

If so, you probaly are the sort of person who believes others are motivated purely by self-interest. But did you know that "cynic" also refers to the school of philosophy particularly associated with Diogenes of Sinope (c. 410–c. 325 B.C.)?

The Cynics favored an extreme form of asceticism and self-sufficiency, believing that morality (and therefore happiness) depended on abandoning the trappings of civilization and returning to the simplicity of nature. Diogenes was legendary for his lack of interest in social niceties and creature comforts, preferring to live in a tub rather than a house. When Alexander the Great asked Diogenes what he would like, the philosopher replied, "You to move out of the sun and not cast a shadow on me." His life was devoted to undermining the artificial values and institutions of a society he considered morally bankrupt.

a man can be considered good, he has first to determine what his function is; only when he has performed his function well will he achieve his goal. Since the function of man—the thing he can do that no other object can—is to reason, and by extension control his desires and conduct *through* reason, there is an ethical or moral side to his search. Virtue is a matter of finding the right balance—the so-called golden mean—between opposing vices.

The value of Aristotle's contribution across the vast range of subjects he considered goes way beyond the doctrines he espoused and the conclusions he reached. It was his clear-sighted, skillful analysis of arguments that made him such an important figure, and it is little wonder that his influence extended through medieval Christian (see Thomas Aquinas, page 70) and Islamic (see Averroes, page 64) philosophy into the modern world.

Epicurus
(341–270 B.C.)

Born to Athenian parents on the island of Samos, Epicurus spent some time teaching in Asia Minor before eventually settling in Athens around 307 B.C. He set up a school known as the Garden, which was—obviously—in his garden, where he taught for the rest of his life. Although only fragments of his work survive, his opinions have come down to us through the writings of his followers, most notably the Roman poet and philosopher Lucretius in his *De Rerum Natura* (*The Nature of Things*).

Known as a hedonist (from the Greek *hēdonē*, "pleasure"), Epicurus held that pleasure is the greatest good, is always good and is to be achieved by avoiding pain. Where pleasure concerns

CAN YOU CALL EPICURUS A HEDONIST TODAY? OR EVEN AN EPICUREAN?

On the one hand, yes, but on the other, no. Hedonism is the ethical doctrine proposing the pursuit of pleasure as the aim of life and is certainly linked with Epicurus.

But of course it all depends on what you mean by pleasure. The aims of a modern hedonist might well differ from those of the followers of Epicurus, for whom pleasure was simply a state of tranquillity achieved through the absence of pain and anxiety.

As to being an epicurean, again, it's all in the name. Today an epicure is someone with a pronounced interest in fine food and wine. Pleasurable, sure, but not in the way that the great man—who was remarkably abstemious—intended.

the body, perfect health is its highest form; where it concerns the mind, freedom from fear and anxiety is the way forward. Although all pleasure is good, some pleasure will inevitably bring with it pain, and this is where wisdom comes into play—wisdom allows people to make the best choice of pleasures.

Epicurus went on to adapt atomism, the theory that everything in the universe is made up of minute particles moving in empty space that was put forward by an earlier philosopher, Democritus. Where Democritus had his atoms coming down in parallel lines, like rain, but colliding every so often in a predetermined sort of way to cause things to change, Epicurus

THE STOICS

It's not a paradox this time...there really was another Zeno. In his early twenties, Zeno of Citium (c. 333–262 B.C.) came to Athens, where he studied for a time at the Academy. He eventually went on to teach at the Stoa Poikile ("Painted Colonnade," which gave its name to his brand of philosophy, Stoicism).

No doubt in response to the prevailing political instability, the Stoics were all for remaining stoical: indifferent to pleasure and pain, to the ups and downs of fortune. Specifically, they believed that the only thing completely within an individual's control was the ability to acquire the correct moral attitude, which could be equated with virtue and was grounded in knowledge. For the Stoics happiness came from knowing the right thing to do in any given circumstance at any given time.

The ideas of the Stoics were taken up and developed over the years, coming to prominence again most notably in Roman times (see Seneca, page 45, and Marcus Aurelius, page 49).

suggested that atoms could swerve for no apparent reason—or that they had free will. He was also a committed empiricist, teaching that all knowledge is ultimately grounded in observation and deduction.

These teachings fed into each other. Once there was no predetermined course of events, no gods controlling what went on in people's lives, one potential cause of anxiety disappeared. Nor should anyone worry about death, since that was the end of consciousness and so would not be felt. Instead, Epicurus set great store by friendship, seeing it as a major ingredient of happiness, and praised simple pleasures—food and shelter—over wealth and political power.

ENTER THE ROMANS

Athens was sidelined politically after defeat by Philip II of Macedon in 338 B.C. With the military exploits of his son Alexander the Great—in twelve short years he overwhelmed the Persian Empire, his armies reaching as far as the Russian steppes, Afghanistan and the Punjab—the balance of power shifted not only within Greece but also to areas beyond.

After Alexander's death in 323 B.C., his conquests were eventually—and acrimoniously—divided among his successors, Antigonus, Ptolemy and Seleucus. They effectively oversaw the creation of the Hellenistic world from their kingdoms in Macedon, Egypt and the vast eastern part of the empire, spreading Greek culture far and wide.

But Rome was beginning to stir; by the middle of the third century B.C., it had gained control of all Italy south of the River Po. From there it extended its interests into Sicily, Corsica and Sardinia, and the rest of the Mediterranean began to look increasingly tempting. By around 200 B.C. the Romans had arguably established a culture of their own, with political systems in place that would develop into the full-blown Roman Republic.

Initially, any Roman wishing to study philosophy headed to Athens, where the various schools of philosophy continued to operate. That situation came to an end in 87 B.C., when the Roman statesman and general Sulla besieged and then sacked Athens. The city was ruined, and a number of its philosophers left, taking their philosophical texts to other centers in the Mediterranean world, including Rome.

There were no exclusively Roman schools of philosophy, which remained a Greek import. Indeed, prior to Lucretius's *De Rerum Natura* (see Epicurus, page 39), there was no philosophical work written in Latin, and Lucretius himself spoke of the difficulty of finding Latin words subtle enough to express the finer points of Epicurean physics. But pre-existing schools of philosophy, in particular Epicureanism and Stoicism, influenced many spheres of Roman life. They contributed to higher education with their emphasis on rhetoric and grammar, and to religion with their analyses of ethics and spirituality. And when the civil wars brought the Republic to a close in 27 B.C. and ushered in the first of the Roman emperors, they even provided a framework to help Republican senators bear their loss of power. So influential was Stoic thought—and obviously also adaptable to a range of political situations—that by the middle of the first century A.D., one of its keenest exponents was tutoring the future emperor Nero, while in the second century it could claim a Roman emperor all for itself (see Marcus Aurelius, page 49).

Seneca

(4 B.C.–A.D. 65)

"That man lives badly who does not know
how to die well."

—*On Tranquillity of Mind*

The Roman Stoic Lucius Annaeus Seneca (the Younger) was born in Cordoba, Spain, the son of a wealthy and well-connected rhetorician and historian. As a young man he studied philosophy and rhetoric in Rome, with a view to pursuing a career in politics. By his thirties he was moving in imperial circles. Having found favor during the reign of Caligula, Seneca was then banished in A.D. 41, accused of committing adultery with Julia, Caligula's sister (and the new emperor Claudius's niece), who by all accounts was something of a wild child. He spent the next eight years in Corsica before being recalled to Rome to act as tutor to the young Nero. When Nero became emperor in 54, Seneca initially retained his influence, even becoming consul three years later—and amassing a considerable fortune in the process. But in the end the notoriously unstable emperor turned against him, and Seneca withdrew from public life in A.D. 62.

Seneca's philosophy is conveyed through his *Moral Essays* and *Moral Epistles to Lucilius*, a series of ten dialogues and 124 letters in Latin in which he gives practical advice on a range of subjects: providence, friendship, the brevity of life, the terrors of death, groundless fears, anger, virtue, the happy life, benefits, clemency, the simple life, tranquillity and so on. Among them are his famous *Consolations*, notably one to

"SENECA CANNOT BE TOO HEAVY..."

So says Polonius in Shakespeare's *Hamlet*, showing that
Elizabethan audiences knew Seneca as a playwright. In
addition to his philosophical works, Seneca wrote eight
big, bloated, gory tragedies: *Hercules Furens*, *The Trojan
Women*, *The Phoenician Women*, *Medea*, *Phaedra*, *Agamemnon*,
Thyestes and *Oedipus*. These were adapted from origi-
nals by Euripides, Aeschylus and Sophocles, but where
the Greek playwrights left violence in the background,
Seneca brought it to the fore, with generous side orders
of revenge and the supernatural, leaving his stage littered
with corpses at the end. Remind you of Shakespeare at all?
Sadly, for Seneca's contemporaries it would probably have
been all too reminiscent of life at Nero's court.

his mother, Helvia, on his exile to Corsica, and another to a woman named Marcia on the death of her sons. Both attempt to show how reason can help someone to bear unhappiness with courage. Throughout all these works self-control is of paramount importance. For Seneca no one can be considered great until they have learned to master themselves and to moderate their desires. Suffering is merely a test that will strengthen an individual, while anger, grief and fear are emotional traps that will enslave them.

Some have suggested that Seneca's Stoicism arose from his struggles to cope with the events that befell him rather than from considered philosophical conviction. It's true that there are contradictions between Seneca the politician and Seneca the Stoic philosopher, the wealthy man at home with emperors who championed the virtues of self-control and the simple life. But his was an attempt to apply philosophy in a practical way, and as tutor to an emperor, he was in a better position than most to try to put his ideas into practice.

Either way, if his life was contradictory, he certainly died in a brave and dignified—not to mention horribly drawn out—fashion. Nero ordered him to commit suicide, so he slit the veins in his arm with a dagger. When that didn't do the trick, he drank poison. Finally, running out of options, he had his servants place him in a bath of boiling water, where he suffocated in the steam.

Epictetus
(55–135)

"But what is philosophy? Does it not mean making
preparation to meet the things that come upon us?"

—*Discourses*

Born a slave in Hieropolis, Phrygia (part of Turkey now),
Epictetus went with his master to Rome, where he studied under
the Stoic teacher Musonius Rufus. At some point he gained his
freedom and began to teach, but in 89 he and other philosophers
were banished from Rome by the emperor Domitian. Epictetus
chose to settle in Nicopolis in northwestern Greece, where he
opened his own highly successful school.

Among his students was the future historian Arrian, who
collected Epictetus's comments on the works of earlier Stoics
into the *Discourses* and the *Handbook*. Written in Greek with a
view to elucidating the philosophical way of life, the *Discourses*—
there were originally eight books, but only four survive—range
over such topics as friendship, illness, fear, poverty, acquiring
and maintaining tranquillity and why it is wrong to be angry
with others. The *Handbook* is a manual of Stoic ethics, illustrated
by everyday examples.

In both works, Epictetus teaches that the purpose of philosophy is to enable the individual to lead a better life, to live
virtuously according to nature and with an awareness of
responsibilities to others, and thus to achieve happiness. The
starting point must be self-examination, with an assessment
of which things in life can be controlled and which cannot,
since unhappiness is caused by worrying about things over

which we have no power. So our opinions are our own—likes and dislikes, judgments and so on—but such things as health, wealth and all forms of public acclaim are beyond our control. The choice is between the freedom that follows when an individual exercises *moral* will and the slavery that results from being misled by the external trappings of success. With discipline and self-knowledge the twin goals of imperturbability (*ataraxia*) and freedom from passion (*apatheia*) in the face of life's upsets will be achieved.

Epictetus's brand of practical Stoicism was addressed not to the ruling elite—even though the emperor Hadrian apparently attended his lectures on occasion—but to a much wider audience: the ordinary people. And they would presumably have found it reassuring at a time when, on the political front, it was becoming increasingly clear that they had little or no power to stand against the might of the imperial machine.

Marcus Aurelius

(121–180)

"Consider that everything which happens, happens justly, and if thou observest carefully, thou wilt find it to be so."

—*Meditations*

A favorite of the emperor Hadrian, Marcus Aurelius was educated by a number of the best teachers in Rome, including the orator Fronto (letters between them survive), and from a young age showed a keen interest in philosophy, especially the works of Epictetus. He was adopted in 138 by Antoninus Pius, who succeeded Hadrian as emperor that year, and then made consul in 140 and again in 145. He carried out his public duties conscientiously while still pursuing his studies in philosophy and law, and became emperor in 161.

Throughout his reign, Marcus Aurelius had to deal with a number of military threats in the northern and eastern parts of the empire. To make matters worse, plague broke out among the eastern armies and then in Rome. While he was off contending with these problems between 170 and 180, the emperor recorded his thoughts on a range of topics from wherever he was encamped. Eventually, what must have started as a private journal written in Greek became the twelve books of the *Meditations*.

The *Meditations* serve as a sort of Stoic self-help manual. For Marcus Aurelius the ultimate aim in life is to live in harmony

---

"TO HIMSELF"

Meditations was not a title used by Marcus Aurelius. In fact, these pieces were not written for or seen by his contemporaries. They first appeared in book form in 1558, published by Andreas Gesner of Zurich, with a Latin translation by Wilhelm Xylander. The original manuscript from which they worked had been in the library of Otto Heinrich, the Elector Palatine, and is now lost. Apparently, it bore the inscription "*ta eis heauton*" ("to himself"), which accurately conveys the fact that Marcus Aurelius was recording private, intimate reflections rather than writing for other people.

ATHENS BACK IN VOGUE AGAIN

With his great interest in philosophy, not to mention his clout as master of the universe, the emperor Marcus Aurelius established four chairs of philosophy in Athens in 177. There was one for each of the main schools— Platonic, Aristotelian, Stoic and Epicurean—and they were endowed with nice fat salaries, too.

with the universe, of which all people are a part and to which they will all return. The way to achieve this is to ignore the distraction of worldly pleasures and aspire instead to self-control, which comes with the use of reason. More important than what people *are* is the way they behave, and they can train themselves to behave better by following Stoic principles. Among the qualities the emperor considers worthy are restraint, simplicity, steadfastness, self-control, submitting to providence, the ability to control anger, and indifference to what cannot be altered.

Writing in 1503, Machiavelli (see page 78) named Marcus Aurelius the last of the Five Good Emperors, praising him for having led a good life and demonstrating such devotion to duty. From the emperor's point of view, his interpretation of Stoic philosophy, with its emphasis on accepting responsibilities, exercising self-control and enduring whatever comes along, must have been particularly comforting during times of war and plague.

Plotinus

(c. 205–70)

Born in Egypt, Plotinus studied philosophy in Alexandria for eleven years before joining the emperor Gordian's expedition against the Persians in 243. He hoped, by doing so, to learn something about Persian and Indian philosophy, but when Gordian was murdered in Mesopotamia, he abandoned his plans and escaped to Antioch (in present-day Turkey). He then made his way to Rome, arriving in 244, and spent most of the rest of his life there teaching philosophy, leaving only shortly before he died.

NEUPLATONISCH?

The term Neoplatonism is not one that would have been recognized in the ancient world. It seems to have come into use in Germany in the mid-nineteenth century, when academics decreed that there was enough new thinking among Plotinus and his followers—who would have considered themselves Platonists—to warrant some sort of distinction.

In 253 Plotinus started writing the treatises that would be collected after his death by his pupil Porphyry and published in about 300 as the *Enneads* (from the Greek *ennea*, "nine," because each of the six books contained nine treatises). These laid the foundations of Neoplatonism, which synthesized the earlier philosophical teachings of Aristotle, the Pythagoreans and the Stoics with those of Plato. Like Plato, Plotinus insists that the intellect is superior to the senses, and the spiritual world to the material. His universe can be divided into a hierarchy of realities, at the top of which is the "One." Transcendental, perfect and complete in itself, the One—which equates with the "Good" in Plato's *Republic*—has no attributes or component parts. It is simply supreme goodness, and it emanates like light from the sun, or indeed overflows, to form the next world down: Intellect. Conceived by the mind of the One, this is the world of ideas and concepts—they equate with Plato's "forms"—and it in turn over-flows into the world of Soul, which is eternal but actively creates and orders the visible universe. From Soul we descend to Nature, peopled with individual souls, and then to the material world, which is the weakest of realities, no longer capable of emanation.

Each individual has within him elements of matter, nature, soul and intellect and must aspire, through contemplation and self-discipline, to reach back up through the hierarchy.

With its fusion of the works of earlier thinkers, Plotinus's Neoplatonism can be seen as the last major contribution to classical philosophy. At the same time, its emphasis on contemplation as a means for lowly humans to commune directly with the One, who sounds remarkably like God, exerted considerable influence on early Christian theology, especially the work of St. Augustine, thus creating a bridge between the ancient and medieval worlds.

CHRISTIANS, MUSLIMS
AND JUST ONE JEW

In 308 there were no fewer than six Roman emperors at the same time, three in the East and three in the West. Sooner rather than later the vast and unwieldy empire was going to split in two. After a fair bit of jostling, the struggle for power in the West came down to a fight between Maxentius and Constantine, who faced each other for the last time at the Milvian Bridge, near Rome, in 312. Here Constantine was victorious against his rival's superior forces. According to legend, he had divine help.

In his *Life of Constantine*, Eusebius—known as the Father of Church History—describes how the night before his great victory, Constantine saw a flaming cross inscribed with the words "In this sign, you will conquer." The sign was the Chi-Rho, the intertwined Greek letters that form the opening of Christ's name. Other writers tell different versions of the story, but everyone agrees that Constantine promptly converted to Christianity. Then, the following year, he and Licinius, who was now emperor in the East, issued the Edict of Milan, which extended religious tolerance to Christians throughout the empire. This was the first time they'd been given official backing. So no more being thrown to the lions....

Fast-forward 300 years or so and another empire, based on another religion, was about to appear on the scene. The prophet Muhammad, founder of Islam, was born in Mecca around 570. At the age of forty, having spent much time in religious contemplation, he began preaching the new faith, based on the Koran (which is often spelled Qur'an or Quran), which had been revealed to him by Allah, the all-powerful, just and compassionate God. Muhammad spoke out against idolatry and superstition, exhorting people to lead a better life through prayer, fasting and almsgiving. He must have been seen as too much of a troublemaker by the authorities, however, because eventually the Meccans rose up against him and his followers. In 622—the date of the Hegira (literally "departure"), which counts as year 1 for Muslims—they fled to Medina, where Muhammad became the chief judge and ruler of the city. From there he embarked on a war against the enemies of Islam, and in 630 he captured Mecca. This time he was recognized as a ruler and prophet of the new religion, which then began to take hold

THE SECOND MASTER

This was the title given to al-Farabi (c. 870–950), the earliest of the Islamic religious philosophers, or *falasifa*, as they were known in Arabic. The title of one of his works, *The Harmonization of the Opinions of the Two Sages: Plato the Divine and Aristotle*, makes his intentions clear. His idea was to come up with a synthesis that incorporated the mystical "One" of Plotinus and the Neoplatonists and the logic and empiricism of Aristotle—the First Master—and then apply it to theology. His approach was hugely influential for later Muslim, Christian and Jewish philosophers.

across Arabia. Muhammad fell ill shortly after returning from his last pilgrimage to Mecca in 632 and died the same year.

His immediate successors, the four Rashidun Caliphs, oversaw a period of military expansion during which Islam was introduced into vast swathes of land that had previously been part of the Roman and Persian empires, with all the ensuing cultural overlap. The Umayyad Caliphs, who came next, continued the expansion through North Africa and into Spain from their capital in Damascus. The following dynasty, the Abbasids, moved the capital from Damascus to the newly founded city of Baghdad, from where they tried to retain control of their rapidly expanding empire from the middle of the eighth century until their eventual conquest by the Mongols in the thirteenth century.

During the heyday of the Abbasids, Baghdad became an intellectual hotbed, home to Muslim and non-Muslim scholars alike.

They oversaw, among other things, the translation into Arabic of works on philosophy, science, medicine and education from the classical world that would otherwise have been lost. Rival Muslim dynasties established themselves throughout the empire, and they also fostered scholarship and intellectual enquiry. Cairo in Egypt under the Fatimids, and Cordoba in Andalusia under the Umayyads became important centers where, in a spirit of tolerance that embraced Christians and Jews, great thinkers from different religious backgrounds were able to flourish.

In the early days of Muslim expansion, Christian Western Europe was intellectually asleep. But in the twelfth century the classical works that had been translated into Arabic in Baghdad and other Islamic centers, most notably the works of Aristotle, retranslated into Hebrew, Greek and Latin, becoming available in the West once more.

So by the Middle Ages the three great monotheistic religions—Judaism, Christianity and Islam—had all come into contact with Greek philosophy. In each case the works of Aristotle were the main point of reference, but there was also an

WHERE ON EARTH?

In the *Republic*, Plato outlined an ideal state ruled by philosopher-kings. Al-Farabi talked of prophet-imams and saw Medina as the perfect city, ruled by Muhammad. For St. Augustine the City of God was a spiritual rather than a geographical place, but the Church was its equivalent on Earth.

interest in Neoplatonism, which both influenced interpretations of Aristotle and staked its own claim for attention. Now the different religious thinkers wanted to apply the thoughts of the ancient philosophers to their own particular theologies.

St. Augustine of Hippo
(354–430)

"Grant me chastity and continence, but not yet."

—*Confessions*

Born in North Africa to a Christian mother and a pagan father, Augustine can be seen as a bridge between classical and Christian philosophy. As a young man, he taught rhetoric in Carthage, which was a thriving intellectual center. While living there, he became involved with Manichaeism—a religious belief system centered on the constant struggle between light and dark/good and evil. He then took up skepticism and Neoplatonism while teaching in Rome and then Milan. It was in Milan in 387 that he converted to Christianity. He was baptized the following year, ordained a priest in 391, and in 396 became the bishop of Hippo (now in Algeria).

Augustine was a prolific author, and his major works, *The Confessions* and *The City of God*, are still read today. For him philosophy and theology were inextricably linked. Once he converted, Christianity became the true philosophy for him, while the pagan beliefs and schools of philosophy he had previously favored were treated as less well-developed theologies—resources to help him elucidate the Christian message.

◎◎ ◎◎ ◎◎

FAITH CAME FIRST WITH AUGUSTINE, AS THE STARTING POINT FROM WHICH TO SEEK WISDOM. BY TRAINING TO BE A TEACHER, HE MOVED FROM TEACHING RHETORIC TO TEACHING CHRISTIANITY, USING HIS OWN LIFE AS AN ILLUSTRATION.

◎◎ ◎◎ ◎◎

From Plato and the Neoplatonists, Augustine took the idea that there is a distinction between the imperfect, transient world of material things, accessed via the senses, and the perfect, eternal world, accessed via the intellect: the City of Men vs. the City of God. This distinction is part of a larger, interlocking hierarchy that starts with absolute unity and then works down through levels of increasing materiality. Absolute unity is God, the ultimate source for all that comes after. Synonymous with Being, Goodness and Truth, God is the fixed point that unifies everything within an eternal, rational hierarchy, and it is to God that individuals must open their minds in order to achieve wisdom and enlightenment.

So how to explain evil in a divinely ordained world? Original sin is to blame. The divine exists within us but has been tarnished by what happened in the Garden of Eden. However, there is a remedy at hand: divine grace. The elect—God's chosen— were predestined to be saved from fiery damnation. This did not detract from individuals' free will to determine their own actions, but God, being present throughout time, the spiritual world being eternal, already knew how they would behave and thus had taken this into account before chosing the elect.

Basically, faith came first with Augustine, as the starting point from which to seek wisdom. By training to be a teacher, he moved from teaching rhetoric to teaching Christianity, using his own life as an illustration and applying his rigorous intellect to a wide range of doctrinal points that he thought needed clarification.

Avicenna
(980–1037)

The foremost physician and philosopher of his day—not to mention child prodigy (he could recite the Koran from memory before the age of ten) and all-around top scholar (he wrote about logic, chemistry, physics, geology, psychology, metaphysics and astronomy, to name but a few)—Ibn Sina is better known in the West by the Latin version of his name, Avicenna. He was born near Bukhara (in modern-day Uzbekistan), where he was educated, and according to his modest autobiography, he had learned all there was to learn by the age of eighteen. He specifically mentions having wrestled with Aristotle's *Metaphysics* for a year and a half, reading it forty times before being satisfied that he fully understood the meaning, thanks to an al-Farabi commentary.

Avicenna's interest in applying Aristotelian and Neoplatonic ideas to Islamic theology is most fully expressed in his major philosophical work, *The Book of Healing*, which covers logic, the natural sciences and metaphysics. Here he talks about the distinction between necessary and contingent being or, in other words, between essence, which just *is*, and existence, which is sort of a hit-and-miss affair—or, put another way, between what something *is* and the form it happens to take. For the essence of anything that exists to take physical form, there has to be a prior cause—

something more powerful, whose own existence is higher in rank. There's a whole hierarchy of existent entities, but at the very top there must surely be something that wasn't caused by anything at all. This is the Necessary Being, in whom essence and existence are identical. In fact, this is God—self-existent and the cause of all other entities.

THE FLOATING MAN

Avicenna asks you to imagine that a fully grown man suddenly comes into being floating in mid-air, blindfolded and limbs splayed. He can see nothing; he is touching nothing. But even without sensation he is aware of his own existence. An early version of "I think, therefore I am"?

Avicenna went against traditional Muslim theologians in rejecting the idea that God created the world from nothing. He argues instead that the world has no beginning but endures as a natural consequence of God's existence as the "One," whose essence is knowledge, will and power. As the uncaused first cause, he is necessarily the creator. Logical or what?

St. Anselm
(1033–1109)

"For this also I believe, that unless I believe,
I shall not understand."

—*Proslogion*

Born in Aosta, Anselm left Italy in 1056 to join the Benedictine abbey of Bec in Normandy, where he studied under Lanfranc, one of the preeminent Church scholars of his day. In 1093 he succeeded Lanfranc as Archbishop of Canterbury and on his death was buried in the cathedral.

Anselm can be seen as the first exponent of scholasticism, which was not so much a philosophy as an approach to learning that used dialectical reasoning to work through questions that arose, so as to resolve apparent contradictions in medieval theology. His aim was to reconcile reason with faith, for while reason was no substitute for faith, it could lead people to an understanding of what they had already accepted through faith.

Anselm is best known for his works setting out proofs for the existence of God. In the *Monologion* he states that in order to be able to call something good, there must necessarily be an objective standard: an absolute good against which we are judging. This absolute is what we call God. In the *Proslogion* he goes further, coming up with his famous ontological argument (not that it was called that until much later): if God is agreed to be the absolute, a being greater than which no other can be conceived, then God must exist in reality, too, because otherwise it would be possible to conceive of another greater something.

It's one of those arguments that make more sense after a bottle of wine or two—and even in Anselm's day it was ridiculed by some scholars. However, over the years it has continued to be discussed by a range of philosophers, including Descartes, Leibniz and Kant (see pages 85, 92, and 106).

Averroes

(1126–98)

"Since philosophy is true and the revealed scriptures
are true, there can be no disharmony between them."
—*On the Harmony of Religions and Philosophy*

The distinguished Islamic philosopher Averroes, or Ibn Rushd, was born in Cordoba into an important family of jurists. He, too, became a judge, first in his home town, then in Seville and finally in Marrakesh, where he died. He wrote on a range of subjects in addition to philosophy, including jurisprudence and medicine, and was at one time physician to the caliph.

In the West he is best known for his thirty-eight commentaries on the works of Aristotle and on Plato's *Republic*. Based on

Arabic translations, some were straightforward summaries, but others included criticism of contributions from later commentators, not only the Neoplatonists but also al-Farabi and Avicenna (see pages 57 and 61). Averroes was intent on getting back to "pure" Aristotelian thought, in part to undermine attacks from Islamic jurists and theologians that he felt were based on misreadings. He wanted to show that there was no conflict between religion and philosophy, that they were merely different ways to reach the same truth. Religious law (*sharia*), being based on faith, could not—and therefore *should* not—be tested, nor did it require special training to understand. Which meant that the theologians, with their dialectical arguments, were merely confusing the issue. As for philosophy, it should be reserved for the elite few who had the intellectual capacity to undertake its study—think Plato and his philosopher-kings.

Having been translated into Hebrew and Latin, the works of Averroes continued to be studied in the West until the middle of the seventeenth century. In the Muslim world, however, his work was condemned by orthodox religious scholars, who rejected his opinion that religious law and philosophy shared the same goal.

Maimonides

(1135–1204)

The Jewish philosopher and Talmudic scholar Maimonides, or Moses ben Maimon—he was also known as Rambam, from the first letters of his name: Rabbi Moshe ben Maimon—was born in Cordoba, where his father was a judge. When he was thirteen, the family left Spain. After several years on the move in North Africa,

Maimonides eventually settled near Cairo in 1165, becoming leader of the Jewish community there. He studied Greek philosophy and medicine and in 1183 was appointed physician to the vizier of the Sultan, Saladin—he of Crusader fame.

Maimonides was a prolific author whose best-known works are his *Guide to the Perplexed*—written originally in Arabic, although later Hebrew and Latin translations reached a much wider audience—and his authoritative fourteen-volume commentary on the Mishnah, or code of Jewish law, the *Mishneh Torah*, which understandably was written in Hebrew. The "perplexed" in question are students of Aristotelian philosophy confused by apparent contradictions between what they are studying and certain statements in the Bible and the Talmud, especially about the nature of God. The aim of the *Guide* is to reconcile Aristotelian philosophy and the Greek sciences with the literal truth of the Old Testament: since all truth is one, the Bible, containing as it does the revealed word of God, can be complementary only to reason. Maimonides explains, for example, that he rejects the Aristotelian view that matter is eternal on the basis of reason,

APOPHATIC THEOLOGY

Bet you can't even say it! But when Maimonides was wrestling with those questions about the nature of God that so perplexed his students, this is what he came up with—and it has to do with negating the attributes that might be applied to God.

Because God's existence is absolute, without composition, we cannot know his essence, only that he exists. Consequently, it is wrong to assume that he has any positive attributes. Negative attributes are necessary to point our minds toward the truths we must believe. So when we say that something exists, what we mean is that its non-existence is impossible; it is living, not dead; it is the first, and its existence has no cause; it has power, wisdom and will and is not weak or ignorant; God is one—there is not more than one God. Every attribute put forward to convey some idea of God's nature denotes the negation of the opposite. Or so says the *Guide to the Perplexed*. Clear now?

not faith. If Aristotle had held the opposing view, Maimonides would have had no difficulty interpreting the biblical creation narrative accordingly.

Despite the fact that he relied on reason, Maimonides believed beyond any shadow of doubt in the Bible as divine revelation. As he saw it, the task of the philosopher was to confirm rationally the truth of religion and to disprove doctrines that seemed to contradict divine revelation.

Roger Bacon

(C. 1214–92)

"There are two ways of acquiring knowledge,
one through reason, the other by experiment."

—*On Experimental Science*

Having studied at the universities of Oxford and Paris, Roger Bacon went on to gain a reputation for learning in a wide range of subjects, including philosophy, mathematics, science and alchemy. Not only did he make full use of the Greek and Arabic texts that had appeared in the West to pursue the recognized route of deductive reasoning, but he also developed the idea of using scientific experimentation to further understanding.

In 1256 he joined the Franciscan Order, the Catholic order founded by St. Francis of Assisi. Around 1266 Pope Clement IV asked Bacon to draw up a program of studies for use in the universities, including the most up-to-date ideas on philosophy, science and language, with a view to improving the Church's teaching of theology and thus its authority. The first part of this undertaking, *Opus maius*, was quickly followed by *Opus minus* and *Opus tertium*.

Bacon distinguishes *experientia*, or experience, from *experimentum*, a set of scientific principles based on experience. Experience is innate, the knowledge of things that all animals have, while scientific principles based on experience have to be learned. And it is scientific principles that allow the discovery of new truths. He outlines experiments in mathematics, astronomy and optics, such as calculating the position of the heavenly bodies, identifying the color spectrum produced by shining

FROM MONKS
TO MODERN UNIVERSITIES

The word "university" is derived from the Latin *universitas magistrorum et scholarium*, meaning a community or corporation of masters and students. Before the formal establishment of universities as self-regulating centers of learning with academic freedom of expression, higher education was based in cathedral or monastic schools, where students were taught by monks and followed patterns of teaching laid down by the Church.

Coinciding with the reintroduction of Aristotle's work to the West, the development of medieval universities saw the beginnings of a wider syllabus more familiar to modern students. Paris (1150) and Oxford (1167), where Roger Bacon and William of Ockham studied, are two of the oldest universities.

◎◎ ◎◎ ◎◎

Bacon distinguishes
***experientia*, or experi-**
ence, from *experimentum*,
a set of scientific
principles based on
experience.

◎◎ ◎◎ ◎◎

light through water, and
writing hypothetically about
telescopes. He even describes
flying machines and suggests
that it might be possible to
power ships and horse-drawn
carriages mechanically.

When Pope Clement
died in 1268, however, the
Church authorities' enthusi-
asm for Bacon's educational methods died with him. Eventually,
Bacon fell from favor with the Franciscans, too. By 1278 they
had become suspicious of his experimental work, condemning
him for what they referred to as "suspected novelties" and possibly even imprisoning him for a while. And that was the end of
Bacon's Church-and-science-working-together experiment.

Thomas Aquinas

(1225–74)

"… for the knowledge of any truth whatsoever
man needs Divine help."

—*Summa Theologica*

Related to the Italian counts of Aquino, Thomas Aquinas was
educated in the Benedictine monastery at Monte Cassino and at
the University of Naples. Against the wishes of his family, who
locked him up for a year to try to dissuade him, he then joined
the Dominicans, a preaching order. He studied and taught in

Cologne and Paris before being summoned to teach in Italy by Pope Alexander IV in 1258. Although once known as the Dumb Ox, presumably because of his build (he was a big man) rather than his intellectual capabilities, he was publishing commentaries on Aristotle by his late twenties. Aquinas wanted to get back to Aristotle in the original, before earlier commentators such as Avicenna and Averroes had reformulated his ideas to fit their own theological frameworks. This was the start of a life spent refining a synthesis of Christian theology and Aristotelian reasoning that in many ways still underpins the doctrines of the Catholic Church.

Aquinas's take on the reason vs. faith argument was that they are separate but complementary, the first subservient without being subordinate. The world is full of real things that we can see and conceive of, but behind them there is a first cause. God's existence could be demonstrated through reason, while specific

---

FIVE (NON-ALCOHOLIC) PROOFS

Using terminology from Aristotle's *Metaphysics*, Aquinas declares that God is the "unmoved mover" who causes change in others (1 = change); the first cause that makes everything else happen (2 = dependence); the one non-contingent, necessary being supporting the existence of all other contingent things (3 = contingency); the greatest being from which lesser beings take whatever greatness they have (4 = limited perfection); the intelligent designer who directs non-intelligent things to act toward an end (5 = utility).

doctrines, such as the Trinity and the incarnation of Christ, were revealed through faith.

Aquinas was the author of two major texts—the *Summa contra Gentiles* (1259–64), a sort of handbook for Dominican missionaries, and the *Summa Theologica* (1266–73), which, though incomplete at the time of his death, laid out all the tenets of his Christian philosophy. The most famous of these is the *quinque viae* ("five ways"), which have become known as his five proofs for the existence of God (see box on page 71).

Aquinas evidently liked systems. As well as the five ways, he gives us five statements about the divine nature of God (he is simple, perfect, infinite, immutable and one), four cardinal virtues (prudence, temperance, justice and fortitude) and three theological virtues (faith, hope and charity).

William of Ockham
(C. 1287–1347)

Born in Ockham, England, William became a Franciscan friar before going on to study theology at Oxford. He never completed his degree or obtained a teaching post, presumably because his views rocked the boat—the chancellor of the university went so far as to accuse him of heresy. As a result, he was summoned to appear before Pope John XXII in Avignon, where he became embroiled in yet more controversy, this time about whether the Franciscans should stick to their vow of poverty. William said yes and the Pope said no—at which point William decided it might be wise to make a hasty exit. He was nonetheless excom-

OCKHAM'S (OR OCCAM'S) RAZOR

An expression that's heard more often than the name William of Ockham (or Occam in Latin). The idea is to use his razor to cut away unnecessary parts of an argument in order to get down to the essentials—more like a potato peeler, really. So if you're faced with conflicting arguments that seem equally valid, go for the one that relies on the fewest assumptions and can be pared down the most.

This is also known as the Law of Parsimony, although it might be better to replace "parsimony" with "pithy" here, because the idea can be boiled down to: The simplest solution is usually the best.

municated and spent the rest of his life under the protection of Emperor Louis IV of Bavaria.

@@ @@ @@

WILLIAM PUT FORWARD THE VIEW THAT THERE ARE NO SUCH THINGS AS OVERARCHING UNIVERSALS, ESSENCES OR FORMS.

@@ @@ @@

In his best-known philosophical work, the *Summa Logicae*, William offers a new take on Aristotle and scholasticism, putting forward the view that there are no such things as overarching universals, essences or forms. Instead, there are just individual objects, and we are made aware of them by our minds through a process referred to as intuitive cognition. When we need to think of several objects at once, we come up with terms such as "universal," but these are only names, nothing more—which explains why William's doctrine is known as nominalism (from the Latin *nomen*, "name"). Each individual object can have component parts, but it is always absolutely singular in itself. None of these individual objects is automatically the cause of another, nor the effect of another, while their coexistence does not alter the fact that they are singular. All of which led him to state, "Plurality is never to be posited without need," which is a fancy way of saying, "Keep things simple," and is the principle behind Ockham's razor (see box, page 73).

William held that there was no way the existence of God could be demonstrated, whatever so-called "proofs" other scholars advanced. But he saw no need to make the link between faith and reason. Faith for him was purely a matter of revelation.

Renaissance Men

Historians tend to go for "Renaissance"—literally, "rebirth"—when they want a word to describe periods marked by a major revival of interest in ideas from antiquity. After the last chapter, it should come as no surprise to learn that there was a twelfth-century Renaissance: it's the term applied to the period of intellectual fervor that followed the rediscovery of Aristotle's works by Christian scholars. But the *real* Renaissance, the cultural one everyone knows about, started in fourteenth-century Italy, from where it spread into other parts of Europe over the course of the fifteenth and sixteenth centuries. Think Giotto, Brunelleschi, Donatello, Leonardo da Vinci and Michelangelo. It had an enormous impact on every area of intellectual life—not just art and architecture but also literature, politics, science, religion and, of course, philosophy. Hence, the expression "Renaissance man" for someone who turns his hand to all manner of intellectual inquiry.

The classical texts that were of interest this time around were literary and historical. Turning away from medieval theology, intellectuals focused more closely on human concerns instead.

They didn't reject Christianity—in fact, quite the reverse, because the Church remained an important patron throughout the period—but the way in which religion was approached began to shift. Realism and human sensibilities assumed much more importance, as in every field of study, which explains the name given to these intellectuals: Humanists. Through a revival of interest in the classical past, coupled with their new approach to learning, Renaissance Humanists attempted to deal with life on Earth rather than focus on the afterlife. Which brings us to Erasmus and Machiavelli, two Renaissance men par excellence.

Desiderius Erasmus

(1466–1536)

"Among the blind the cross-eyed man is king."

—*Adages*

Born in Rotterdam, Desiderius Erasmus was the son of a priest who had spent time in Italy studying Greek and Latin and no doubt soaking up all that Renaissance spirit before returning to his parish in the Netherlands. Erasmus was educated in Deventer at one of the top Latin secondary schools in the country, and later in 's-Hertogenbosch, at a school run by the Brethren of the Common Life—an association founded a century earlier to promote Christian values and worship. He was encouraged to join the Augustinian monastery at Steyn, near Gouda, which he did in 1487, and was ordained in 1492.

It must have been pretty obvious that Erasmus didn't want to stay in the monastery, however, because he immediately took a post with the Bishop of Cambrai, leaving him shortly afterward to study theology and then teach in Paris. Here he came face to face for the first time with people who had been exposed to the full range of Humanist ideas spreading out from Italy. As a young man, he had questioned the constraints of traditional medieval scholasticism, but now in Paris he could give full rein to his wider interests. He embarked on a life of scholarship that would see him teaching across Europe, corresponding with leading thinkers of the day— such men as John Colet and Thomas More, for example—and publishing widely, thanks to that wonderful new invention, the printing press.

Erasmus had no intention of breaking with the Catholic Church, but he wanted to apply critical reasoning to its teachings and practices. He spoke out against Church leaders' reliance on superstition and tradition to keep people in line, arguing instead for a return to a simpler, more rational piety based on a clear understanding of the Scriptures—he produced his own translation of the New Testament in Greek with this in mind. His best-known work, though, is *The Praise of Folly*—dedicated to Thomas More—in which he satirizes, among other things, some of the worst excesses of contemporary bishops, priests and monks: their worldliness, ignorance, greed and immorality, just for starters.

Erasmus's criticisms reflected prevailing dissatisfaction with the Church and were taken up by such reformers as Martin

> **ERASMUS HAD NO INTENTION OF BREAKING WITH THE CATHOLIC CHURCH, BUT HE WANTED TO APPLY CRITICAL REASONING TO ITS TEACHINGS AND PRACTICES.**

Luther, but while Luther ultimately split the Church and ushered in the Protestant Reformation, Erasmus tried to keep out of the increasingly acrimonious religious disputes to which his writings contributed.

Niccolò Machiavelli
(1469–1527)

"It is much safer to be feared than loved when,
of the two, either must be dispensed with."

—*The Prince*

Someone who didn't advocate keeping out of disputes was the Florentine political philosopher Niccolò Machiavelli. Little is known about his early life, but in 1498 he was appointed to two administrative posts: secretary of the Second Chancery and secretary to the Council of Ten, which handled foreign affairs for the Florentine Republic. He took part in a number of diplomatic missions over the next fourteen years, in the course of which he met many of the most important political leaders of the time, including Louis XII of France, the Holy Roman emperor Maximilian I, Pope Julius II and Cesare Borgia. His reports and letters make it clear that he studied these people and their actions with considerable enthusiasm and insight, and it was surely during this time that he developed the ideas that later appeared in his best-known work, *The Prince*.

The return in 1512 of the Medici, the previous rulers of Florence in practice if not in name, meant the end of both the republic and Machiavelli's diplomatic career. To make matters

WAS MACHIAVELLI MACHIAVELLIAN?

Although he was also a historian, playwright and poet, Machiavelli is best known for *The Prince*, which explains why the word "Machiavellian" is applied to someone who is cunning, scheming and unscrupulous, especially in the political sphere.

worse, the following year, he was accused of conspiracy and tortured. Although he was pardoned, Machiavelli withdrew from public life and devoted himself to writing.

In the form of a letter to Lorenzo de' Medici, *The Prince* (1513, but not published until 1532) was intended as a handbook for rulers, with advice on what a prince should say and do to achieve and retain political power. Where, in the past, political theorists might have been concerned with how to promote the common good and act justly, Machiavelli was more interested in exploring the ways in which rulers could keep a tight grip on their position. And if murder was the most logical tack, so be it—getting rid of the previous ruling family was crucial.

The Prince advocates cruelty if it makes your subjects frightened of you and therefore malleable, but it should be swift and emphatic. Rewards, however, should be offered sparingly, to keep them wanting more. Deception must be practiced because people are superficial, but rulers should always *pretend* to be virtuous, so as not to give their subjects any grounds for hatred.

In essence *The Prince* says that rulers must be prepared to do bad things if they judge that the results will be worth it: the ends justify the means and so on. This shift from idealism to realism is Machiavelli's great contribution to political philosophy.

THE AGE OF REASON

All those certainties of the past—one Church, with the king ruling by divine right as God's representative on Earth—had broken down big-time by the seventeenth century. In England civil war raged between Royalists and Parliamentarians, culminating in the king losing his head, and throughout Europe there was ongoing conflict between Catholics and Protestants. The nature of the monarchy and the relationship between ruler and ruled were very much up for discussion. Fortunately, the fact that such thinkers as Hobbes and Locke (see pages 82 and 88) often had to flee to other countries just to stay out of harm's way didn't prevent them from producing major works of political philosophy that are still in print today.

The detachment of philosophy from theology was well under way during this period. It's not that the existence of a deity was in doubt, but blind faith was never going to be enough again. Arguments had to be put forward and supported, and in the seventeenth century there was an awful lot of interest in two main approaches to philosophy: rationalism and empiricism.

In the rationalist camp were those who argued that reason—logical, mathematical, if-A-then-B reasoning—could provide the basis for all knowledge: Descartes, Spinoza and Leibniz (see pages 85, 90, 92) were the main players. In the empiricist camp were those who believed that knowledge could come only through the senses, from experience: enter Hobbes and Locke (see below and page 88), with their reliance on experiments in the natural sciences.

Thomas Hobbes

(1588–1679)

"The life of man [is] solitary, poor, nasty,
brutish, and short."

—*Leviathan*

Born in Malmesbury, England—prematurely, when his poor mother heard that the Spanish Armada was on its way, or so he liked to tell people—Thomas Hobbes was educated at Oxford and then worked as a tutor, mainly to members of the aristocracy. In this capacity he traveled widely, meeting many of the leading intellectual figures of the day, including Galileo and Descartes (see page 85).

At the age of forty, Hobbes became fascinated by Euclidean geometry and the idea that its certainties might be applicable to a study of people and society—in other words, that there might be similar rules governing political science. And when, just as Parliament was flexing its democratic muscles against Charles I, Hobbes reached the conclusion, in his *Elements of Law Natural and Political*, that monarchy was the best form of government, he decided that exile was the wisest course and fled to France. He remained in France for eleven years, until 1651, even tutoring the future Charles II while there.

In 1642 Hobbes completed *De Cive* ("About the Citizen"), in which he first put forward his ideas on the origins of civil society. It was not translated into English until 1651, by which time he had fleshed out these ideas into his major work, *Leviathan: The Matter, Forme, and Power of a Commonwealth Ecclesiasticall and*

WHAT A BEAST

Leviathan is the name of the beast from the depths, the great sea monster referred to in the Book of Job. Hobbes himself was dubbed the Beast of Malmesbury by opponents.

Civil (1651), with reflections on metaphysics, psychology and political philosophy.

After his visit to Galileo in 1636, Hobbes had incorporated the science of mechanics and motion into his thinking as a way to explain human behavior. A materialist, he believed the world to be a purely mechanical system made up of nothing but matter in motion, driven by forces of attraction and repulsion under the laws of nature. These forces governed human behavior and determined what people considered "good" (attractive) and "bad" (repulsive). Because humans are wholly selfish in the state of nature, they fight each other for what they need, which can lead only to war and the unpleasant state of life noted in the quotation at the start of this entry. To avoid this, in a spirit of enlightened self-interest, humans agree to a social contract whereby each surrenders a bit of independence for the greater good. The resulting civil society exists under a sovereign with absolute power, to whom everyone agrees to defer in return for protection from war. Only if he fails to deliver on the protection front should the sovereign expect trouble. Otherwise, in order to be effective, he has every right to total control of civil, military, judicial and ecclesiastical matters.

Hobbes must have known his views would offend all sorts of people. His support for the monarchy upset Parliamentarians, and by denying the divine right of kings, he upset many Royalists (although interestingly not Charles II himself, who always had a soft spot for his old tutor). Accusations of atheism against him led some clergymen to recommend burning not only his books but Hobbes himself. Once again, Charles II stepped in to protect him.

René Descartes

(1596–1650)

"I think, therefore I am."

—Discourse on Method

René Descartes was born in France at La Haye en Touraine, which was subsequently renamed La Haye Descartes in his honor. Educated at the Jesuit college of La Flèche in Anjou, he would have had a thorough grounding in the scholasticism he was later to question. Descartes then studied law at Poitiers, but rather than practicing, he opted to reflect on life for a while, so he went to the Dutch Republic in 1618 and enlisted in the army of Maurice of Nassau. The following year, while serving in Germany, he had a series of visions that showed him how the whole of philosophy—and knowledge in general—could be recast as a unified system of truths based on mathematics and

---

CARTESIAN COORDINATES

In his spare time Descartes was a mathematician of note. Anyone who's ever wrestled with graph paper in a math lesson, plotting x and y coordinates, has René to blame. His system allows you to locate points on a plane by means of paired coordinates, which also means you can express geometric shapes as algebraic equations...if you want to. It might not be much fun in class, but it comes in very handy when map reading.

supported by rationalism. In 1628, after ten more years reflecting his way around Europe, Descartes settled in Holland, where he spent most of the rest of his life. It was here that he wrote his major works, *Discourse on Method* (1637), *Meditations on First Philosophy* (1641) and *Principles of Philosophy* (1644).

TAKE THE WAX TEST

Hold a piece of wax to a candle flame and it will change texture, shape and size. Is it still wax? Yes, even though it looks and feels quite different. "And so," Descartes says, "something which I thought I was seeing with my eyes is in fact grasped solely by the faculty of judgment which is in my mind" (*Meditations on First Philosophy*).

The starting point for Descartes is the quest for certainties—never an easy matter, he realizes, as the senses can be deceived. The method he proposes to use is known as hyperbolic doubt—"hyperbolic" in the sense of "extreme." To test how grounded in reason our so-called "knowledge" is, we need to suspend judgment on any proposition whose truth can in any way be doubted. By a process of elimination, Descartes arrives at his famous conclusion, *Cogito, ergo sum* ("I think, therefore I am"). He is certain of his own existence; otherwise, he would not be thinking.

Descartes then takes a look at *what* he is thinking, identifying among other things the idea of a Perfect Being, or God. He is sure that this is true and must exist outside his mind, because otherwise the *cogito* itself would not be true. Which sounds like scholasticism again, although this time the Perfect Being helps prove the reliability of human reasoning: he is God "in whom all the wisdom of the sciences lies hid." Since God leads Descartes to believe that things in the external world are material, they must be, because a perfect God would not deceive him. And just as in the wax test (see box, opposite), it is reason rather than perception that tells Descartes he can trust the evidence of his senses. This dualism—Cartesian dualism, no less: the split between the non-material, thinking mind and the material, mechanistic body—continues to interest people to this day.

When Queen Christina of Sweden decided in 1649 that she wanted philosophy lessons, she summoned Descartes. The venture was not a success. Christina liked to start at five in the morning, even though it was the middle of winter and he preferred a quiet morning in bed, reading and reflecting. He died of pneumonia within six months of arriving.

John Locke

(1632–1704)

"… we can have knowledge no further
than we have ideas."

—*An Essay Concerning Human Understanding*

Born in Somerset, England, John Locke was educated at Oxford, where he found himself completely out of step with what he considered the obsolete scholastic philosophy of the time. Instead, he was much more interested in the experiments in physics and chemistry being carried out in Oxford at the time by people such as Robert Boyle—he of Boyle's law, the one about the relationship between the pressure and volume of a gas— and the study of medicine. In 1667 he joined the household of prominent politician Lord Ashley as a doctor and adviser in scientific and political affairs, coming into contact with leading figures in London as a result. When Ashley became the first Earl of Shaftesbury and Charles II's Lord Chancellor in 1672, Locke was given a government position, but he retired and moved to France in 1675, ostensibly for reasons of health but possibly on political grounds, too. In 1683 he went to Holland,

---

CREDIT CRUNCH

Locke wasn't just a philosopher. His snappily titled *Some Considerations on the Consequences of the Lowering of Interest and the Raising of the Value of Money* (1691) could teach the bankers of today a thing or two.

where he became involved with English supporters of William of Orange, and did not return to England until after the Glorious Revolution of 1688, which saw William of Orange and his wife, Mary, crowned William III and Mary II.

In his *Two Treatises of Government* (1690), Locke sets out his political philosophy, which provides justification for the revolution. He disputes the traditional idea that kings have a divine right to rule as God's representatives on Earth and takes the social contract a step further than Hobbes by incorporating the sovereign. In a state of nature, before anyone has even thought about coming together to form a government, people have the right to defend their life, their health and their property. In order to settle disputes about such matters, they agree to form a government that will protect their rights. But that government rules *only* with the consent of the governed; should it fail to look after their rights, it loses its legitimacy and can justifiably be overthrown.

Locke's major philosophical work, *An Essay Concerning Human Understanding* (1690), was some twenty years in the making. Our minds, he says, are like blank canvases to begin with; we have no innate ideas. But once we start to sense things, the first simple ideas come, and from these "ideas of sensation" we move on to "ideas of reflection"—knowledge that results from reflecting on our sensory experiences. So consciousness, perception and thought all spring ultimately from experience. Which makes Locke an empiricist: someone who believes that knowledge is based on experience derived from the senses. And this harks right back to his early belief in the value of scientific experimentation.

Baruch Spinoza

(1632–77)

"A free man is one who lives under the guidance
of reason, who is not led by fear, but who directly
desires that which is good."

—*Ethics*

The Dutch philosopher also known as Benedictus de Spinoza
(Baruch and Benedictus both mean "blessed" in Hebrew and
Latin, respectively) was born in Amsterdam into a Jewish family
that had fled Portugal to escape persecution. Religion obviously
remained problematic, because in 1656 he was expelled from the
Jewish community, his freethinking approach too much for the
synagogue authorities.

By trade Spinoza was a lens grinder and polisher, and that's
how he made his living, but he devoted his life to the study of
ideas, corresponding over many years with other scientific and
philosophical writers. As his fame spread, a society was formed
to discuss his works, and from 1663 his home near The Hague
was a meeting place for leading intellectuals of the day. That
same year, he published *The Principles of Descartes' Philosophy*, the
only work to appear under his name during his lifetime. In 1673
he turned down the chance to teach philosophy at Heidelberg
University because he wanted the freedom to continue his own
research. He died of consumption four years later, possibly
because of all the glass powder he'd inhaled.

Spinoza's views on religion first appeared in print in his
Theologico-Political Treatise, which was published anonymously
in 1670 and banned in 1674, having offended the religious

authorities. Here he suggests that the Bible should be interpreted by careful study alone, rather than with a view to supporting preconceived ideas or doctrines, and acknowledges that this might reveal many beliefs about God and the universe to be false. What's more, he says that God acts only according to the laws of his own nature, not with any particular purpose in mind. His ideas led to an argument for religious tolerance, which made him unpopular in certain quarters.

Even more controversial was the *Ethics* (1677), which could not be published until after Spinoza's death. Each of its five parts is treated like a mathematical problem, opening with a set of definitions and axioms from which Spinoza deduces theorems, or proofs. Rejecting Descartes's mind–body dualism, he concludes that there is only one substance, which is both God and nature. This amounts to pantheism: the belief that God can be identified with nature and nature is a manifestation of God. For Spinoza nature is both infinite and perfect. Everything, including human beings, is an aspect of nature, which operates—again—according to its own necessity. This means there's no such thing as chance or free will; anyone who thinks they have free will just doesn't understand the causes determining their actions. Nor is there any objective good or evil—such things depend on your viewpoint. Happiness will never be achieved by acquiring possessions or through the

@@ @@ @@

FOR SPINOZA
THE FUNDAMENTAL PHILO-
SOPHICAL QUESTIONS ARE
TO BE ANSWERED NOT BY
EXPERIMENT BUT THROUGH
THE USE OF REASON—
WHICH MAKES HIM A
RATIONALIST.

@@ @@ @@

emotions. A life of reason is the only way forward, and the greatest good comes from knowledge of God.

For Spinoza, then, the fundamental philosophical questions are to be answered not by experiment but through the use of reason—which makes him a rationalist.

Gottfried Wilhelm Leibniz
(1646–1716)

"Nothing happens without a sufficient reason,
why it should be so, rather than otherwise."
—Letter to Samuel Clarke, *A Collection of Papers,*
Which passed between the late Learned Mr. Leibnitz,
and Dr. Clarke, In the Years 1715 and 1716

Born in Leipzig, Germany, where his father was professor of moral philosophy at the university, Gottfried Wilhelm Leibniz started his studies there at the age of fourteen. He graduated in 1663 and then studied jurisprudence for three years, publishing a paper on legal education that impressed the elector of Mainz, for whom he went to work.

The elector was eager to explore ways of keeping the peace in Europe—these were troubled times, with France looking aggressively in Germany's direction—so Leibniz set to work defining a rational foundation for Christianity that would suit both Catholics and Protestants, thus encouraging religious tolerance. Having gone on a diplomatic mission to Louis XIV, Leibniz stayed in France for four years, mixing with leading intellectuals, and also visited London, where he was elected a member of the

Royal Society. In 1676, when the elector of Mainz died, Leibniz became librarian to the Duke of Brunswick at Hanover. On his way back to Hanover, he visited Spinoza (see page 90), who had just completed the *Ethics*. For the rest of his life, Leibniz carried out his court duties while compiling a history of the

THE INVISIBLE COLLEGE

It sounds like Harry Potter, but this was the name given by Robert Boyle to the group of natural scientists who met regularly to exchange ideas and discuss their experiments. The college was the precursor to the Royal Society, which was founded in London in 1660. Leibniz went there to demonstrate the calculating machine he had designed and built. A large metal contraption operated by cranks and dials, Leibniz's Stepped Reckoner was the first machine of its kind to not only add and subtract but also multiply and divide.

House of Brunswick and developing his own work, which now exists mainly in the form of unpublished papers and letters.

In *Theodicy* (1710), one of his few books, Leibniz discusses how to reconcile the existence of an all-powerful, benevolent God with the fact of general unpleasantness in the world. He invokes the sufficient-reason principle, which holds that everything has a reason to exist, and to exist in just the way it does. So in the case of God deciding what sort of world to create, he must have had sufficient reason for creating the one we're living in. And because God is morally perfect, his choice must have been determined by the value of our world. Which in turn means that our world must be the best possible.

The late work *Monadology* (1714) contains Leibniz's conclusions about the composition of the universe. It is made up, he says, of ultimate substances called monads (from the Greek *monos*, "alone"), each of which is eternal and incorruptible. Despite appearances to the contrary, these monads do not interact with each other causally—cause and effect are illusions, as are space and time. Rather, each monad is busy following pre-programmed instructions and behaves as it does purely because that is part of its identity: a monad is "pregnant" with the future and "laden" with the past, just like a seed.

Leibniz wrote widely on a range of subjects—history, law and political theory, for starters—and made major contributions to the study of mathematics. He and Isaac Newton both claimed to have developed calculus; then there was his calculating machine (see box on page 93), not to mention work on statistics and probability theory. He saw the logic inherent in mathematics as the way to refine philosophical reasoning and check objectively for mistakes in arguments—the perfect way to settle disputes rationally.

THE AGE OF
ENLIGHTENMENT

A massive outpouring of intellectual, scientific and cultural activity in the eighteenth century both fostered and was fed by a range of philosophical ideas, all of which competed with each other in applying the analytical methods Isaac Newton had used so successfully in the natural world to the study of mankind. The sense that the dark clouds of ignorance could be dispelled by a rigorous questioning of traditional values explains why the period is known as the Age of Enlightenment. From now on, reason was to be the only yardstick, and who better to come up with a systematic approach than philosophers?

Unsurprisingly, different philosophers reached different conclusions based on their own definitions of reason, so enlightenment took many forms, and it is clear that momentous ideas were being discussed. Freedom and democracy were up for discussion, plus further questioning of religious beliefs and authority. Taken together with ideas about the contractual basis of rights, these concepts would lead to all sorts of political upheavals, including the American and French revolutions.

There was no going back. As Kant said in an essay entitled "Answering the Question: What is Enlightenment?" (1784), "Enlightenment is man's emergence from his self-incurred immaturity." His rallying cry was: "Dare to know!"

George Berkeley
(1685–1753)

"... *esse* is *percipi* [to be is to be perceived]."
—*A Treatise Concerning the Principles of Human Knowledge*

Born near Kilkenny, Ireland, George Berkeley was educated at Trinity College Dublin, becoming a fellow there in 1707. He was ordained a deacon in 1709 and a priest the following year.

Berkeley's most important philosophical works were published relatively early in his life: *Essay towards a New Theory of Vision* in 1709, *A Treatise Concerning the Principles of Human Knowledge* in 1710 and *Three Dialogues between Hylas and Philonous* in 1713. He visited London in 1713, then spent several years traveling in Italy and France. When he returned to Ireland in 1721, he wrote the anonymous *Essay towards Preventing the Ruin of Great Britain*, "an attack on luxury both as an economic and as a political and moral evil." Around the same time, he became wildly enthusiastic about the idea of establishing a university in Bermuda to train that colony's ministers and missionaries to spread the gospel "among the American savages"—no doubt to prevent ruin there, too. He was made Dean of Derry in 1724,

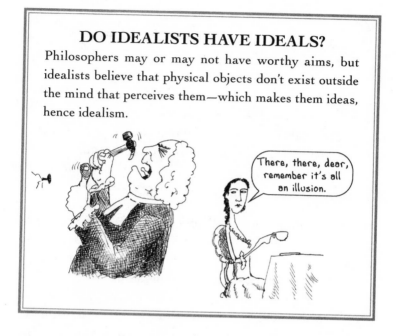

DO IDEALISTS HAVE IDEALS?

Philosophers may or may not have worthy aims, but idealists believe that physical objects don't exist outside the mind that perceives them—which makes them ideas, hence idealism.

and after lobbying in London to get support for his project, he and his new wife sailed west in 1728. They settled temporarily in Rhode Island to await the promised funds, but these never materialized. After three years he abandoned his dream, returning home, and in 1734 he was made Bishop of Cloyne.

Berkeley was not only an empiricist but also a leading idealist. He was deeply troubled, therefore, by the scope of skepticism and atheism espoused by John Locke (see page 88), with its emphasis on materialism: skepticism because the senses can mislead about the nature of material things, which might not even exist in the first place; atheism because it's possible for a material world to work without divine involvement.

FROM BERMUDA TO BERKELEY

In 1968 the College of California and the Agricultural, Mining, and Mechanical Arts College merged to create the University of California. And who did the authorities decide to name their university after? The good bishop, of course, thanks to his enlightened ideas about colonial education. So Berkeley got his university, after all.

The way forward came to Berkeley like a revelation: he denied the existence of matter. So taking the example of an apple, "a certain color, taste, smell, figure and consistence having been observed to go together, are accounted one distinct thing, signified by the name apple"—that's all an apple is. And does it still exist if no one perceives it? Well, Berkeley's answer was that, thanks to the existence of an omnipresent God, the apple was always being perceived. And what causes ideas in the first place? That's God again, because only God, being omni-scient, could manage such an undertaking. As to what becomes of scientific theories if matter is denied, the answer is straightforward enough: they apply to the world of our experience, enabling us to predict outcomes, and that's all—they don't exist beyond our minds.

On a less spiritual level, one of Berkeley's most popular works—a bestseller in his lifetime—was *Siris* (1744), in which with evangelical zeal he spread the word about the medicinal benefits of tar water, a miracle cure for all ailments.

Voltaire

(1694–1778)

"Doubt is not a pleasant condition.
But certainty is an absurd one."
—Letter to Frederick the Great, November 28, 1770

François-Marie Arouet was born in Paris and educated by Jesuits at the Collège Louis-le-Grand. From his early twenties his satirical writings got him into trouble, leading to periods of banishment from Paris and even imprisonment in the Bastille. It was during one prison stay that he adopted the name Voltaire. In 1726 he was let out of prison on the condition that he leave for England immediately, and he spent the next three years there, mixing with leading literary and political figures of the day. He was captivated by the concepts of civil liberties and constitutional monarchy he encountered, and also with the empirical approach taken by John Locke (see page 88) and Isaac Newton, who were to provide him with a rational framework to challenge what he saw as superstition and ignorance in his own country.

Voltaire had already produced poems, plays and essays, but from this time on, his writing took a more overtly philosophical turn. Back in Paris he started work on his *Philosophical Letters on the English Nation* (1734), which conveyed his admiration for the liberal attitudes he'd come across in England. These stood in marked contrast to the norms in France, with its absolute monarch, entrenched aristocracy and pronounced religious intolerance. Devoting himself to challenging the power of the establishment—his book led to more threats against him—he retreated to the country to avoid arrest. In 1750 he left France for the Prussian court at the request of Frederick

THE WORLD ACCORDING TO PANGLOSS

As Dr. Pangloss tells Candide, "things cannot be otherwise than as they are; for all being created for an end, all is necessarily for the best end. Observe, that the nose has been formed to bear spectacles—thus we have spectacles. Legs are visibly designed for stockings—and we have stockings." Even the fact that he has contracted syphilis doesn't diminish his optimism, "for if Columbus had not in an island of America caught this disease, which contaminates the source of life, frequently even hinders generation, and which is evidently opposed to the great end of nature, we should have neither chocolate nor cochineal." So that's all right, then.

the Great, and although the two fell out after a few years, their correspondence continued.

Voltaire made his next home in Switzerland, settling near Geneva in 1755, and it was while living there that he published *Candide* (1759). The novel satirizes the philosophy of Leibniz (see page 92) through the mouth of Dr. Pangloss, Candide's tutor, who assures his charge that absolutely everything—earthquake, war, rape, murder, you name it—happens for the best "in this best of all possible worlds" (see box, above).

Voltaire was a deist—a believer in the existence of a supreme being—rather than a Christian, having seen too much of the damage organized religion could cause. His *Philosophical Dictionary* (1764) contained entries that argued once more against the Church for its encouragement of superstition, repression and intolerance, and advocated freedom of expression.

A prolific writer, a constant thorn in the side of Church and State, and a champion of reason, Voltaire embodied the Enlightenment, while his ideas were to influence the French Revolution, which was just around the corner.

David Hume
(1711–76)

"The great advantage of the mathematical sciences above the moral consists in this, that the ideas of the former, being sensible, are always clear and determinate."

—*An Enquiry Concerning Human Understanding*

Born in Edinburgh, David Hume studied at the university there, took up and abandoned a career in law, worked as a clerk in Bristol and then, in 1734, went off to La Flèche in France, where Descartes (see page 85) had been educated. He stayed three years, studying and working on his first and most important book, *A Treatise of Human Nature* (1739–40), before returning eventually to Scotland. The book's subtitle, *An Attempt to Introduce the Experimental Method of Reasoning into Moral Subjects*, makes it clear that Hume intended to take to its logical conclusion the work of earlier empiricists such as Locke and Berkeley (see pages 88 and 96), rooting out any explanations that depended on "invention [rather] than experience." He divided his *Treatise* into three sections—"Of the Understanding," "Of the Passions" and "Of Morals"—which among them encompassed his ideas on perception, causation, identity and ethics as they related to individuals and society. However, despite its sweeping ambition, the book fell on deaf ears when it first appeared.

THE SUN WILL COME OUT TOMORROW—MAYBE

Reasoning, said Hume, is about discovering relationships between things. He identified two different sorts: "relations of ideas" and "matters of fact." That 15 is half of 30, for example, can be discovered and demonstrated by reason alone, without reference to other forms of evidence, so it belongs in the first category. Statements such as "The sun will rise tomorrow," however, cannot be demonstrated by reason alone; as long as their negation is conceivable, we depend on experience to determine whether they are true or false—which means they belong in the second category.

Undeterred, Hume went on to produce *Essays Moral and Political* (1741–2), which had an immediate impact, and his literary reputation began to grow. A reworking of the *Treatise*, now entitled *An Enquiry Concerning Human Understanding* (1748) and *An Enquiry Concerning the Principles of Morals* (1751), followed. He also published a six-volume *History of England* (1754–62). Accused of being an atheist in his lifetime, Hume delayed publication of his last philosophical work, *Dialogues Concerning Natural Religion*; it was not published until 1779.

◎◎ ◎◎ ◎◎

THE MIND, HUME SAYS, CONSISTS OF PERCEPTIONS, OF WHICH THERE ARE TWO KINDS: IMPRESSIONS, WHICH ARE FORCEFUL AND LIVELY, AND IDEAS, WHICH ARE FAINT COPIES OF THEM.

◎◎ ◎◎ ◎◎

Hume's main arguments appear in the *Treatise*. The mind, he says, consists of perceptions, of which there are two kinds: impressions (sensations, passions and emotions), which are forceful and lively; and ideas (thinking and reasoning), which are faint copies of them. We cannot say that these impressions represent real objects, because we have no real objects to compare them with. We might *think* we live in a world of objects that exist in time and space, ordered by causal laws, but that's just the result of custom and habit, with past experience determining what we expect to see. As for the passions, they are what make us act, preceding reason every time. What's more, ethical or moral certainties cannot be deduced from descriptions of things as, say, good or bad; these are just personal assessments. It is only because such skepticism is not a helpful way to live that, for practical purposes, we agree that our senses are telling us about real things.

Rather than going on from this position to suggest some form of ultimate reality, Hume put forward a naturalist, non-metaphysical account—no supreme being, no first principles—based solely on experience and observation. Although he was more famous in his lifetime as a historian, his attempts to clarify how we know what we know have had a major influence on subsequent philosophers.

Jean-Jacques Rousseau
(1712–78)

"Man is born free; and everywhere he is in chains."
—*The Social Contract*

Born in the Calvinist (strictly Protestant) city of Geneva, Jean-Jacques Rousseau had an unsettled childhood. His mother died just a few days after his birth, and ten years later his father fled to avoid imprisonment, leaving Rousseau to be brought up by an uncle. He had little formal education and left Geneva in 1728, wandering round Italy and Savoy before finally moving to Paris in 1742.

Here Rousseau made his living as a secretary and music copyist. After writing his own opera, he came to the attention of Voltaire (see page 99) and then Denis Diderot (see box, opposite), as a result of which he contributed entries to the *Encyclopédie* on music (1749) and then political economy (1755). In a prizewinning essay of 1750, *Discourse on the Arts and Sciences*, Rousseau argued that advancements in these areas,

KNOW IT ALL

In 1745 the Parisian publisher and printer André le Breton decided to have Ephraim Chambers' Cyclopaedia (1728) translated from English into French. After several false starts Denis Diderot became chief editor of the *Encyclopédie ou Dictionnaire Raisonné des Sciences, des Arts et des Métiers*. Between 1751 and 1765 seventeen volumes were published, with entries on every branch of knowledge, including philosophy, mathematics, politics and religion. Many of the best-known figures of the French Enlightenment contributed, including Voltaire and Rousseau (see pages 99 and 104).

rather than being beneficial, corrupted people's natural goodness and limited their freedom, while in *Discourse on the Origin and Basis of Inequality Among Men* (1754) he developed his theme that people are essentially good, not to mention free, when in a state of nature, but are corrupted and made unhappy by their experiences in society. These ideas were to reappear in his most important work of political philosophy, *The Social Contract* (1762).

In it Rousseau argues for an arrangement—the contract of his book's title—whereby, in return for the protection given by society, individuals surrender their natural rights to the collective "general will." Sovereignty, which for Rousseau means the power to make laws, resides in this general will of the people and so can only represent the common good. The resulting laws are then enacted by the government. Liberty and equality will automatically follow for all, as the general will protects one person against the will of another, while laws that have been made collectively cannot impinge on individual freedoms (though it is made clear that anyone who disagrees will "be forced to be free"—in their own best interests, of course). Rousseau did concede that the kind of republican government he was advocating would work best in a small city-state—somewhere like Geneva, for example—rather than a large country, but the idea of the state having a collective, over-riding will of its own is one that's been accepted by many a large country since.

Rousseau's ideas about education were also to be very influential. In his book *Emile* (1762), he recommends that children's natural tendencies should be encouraged to develop rather than curbed or disciplined, and that learning should come from example rather than from books or lectures. Which is quite odd once you know that Rousseau abandoned his five children to foundling hospitals.

Immanuel Kant
(1724–1804)

"Act only on that maxim whereby thou canst at the same time will that it should become a universal law."
—*Groundwork of the Metaphysic of Morals*

The son of a saddler, Immanuel Kant was born in Königsberg, East Prussia, and lived there or nearby his whole life. He studied at the university, where he then taught as a lecturer, before becoming Professor of Logic and Metaphysics in 1770. Renowned for his quiet and orderly way of life (see box on page

WHAT'S THE TIME, MR. KANT?

According to Heinrich Heine, in his book *On the History of Religion and Philosophy in Germany* (1832), "I do not believe that the great clock of the cathedral [in Königsberg] performed in a more passionless and methodical manner its daily routine than did its townsman, Immanuel Kant. Rising in the morning, coffee-drinking, writing, reading lectures, dining, walking, everything had its appointed time, and the neighbors knew that it was exactly half-past three when Immanuel Kant stepped forth from his house in his grey, tight-fitting coat, with his Spanish cane in hand, and betook himself to the little linden avenue called to this day Philosopher's Walk.

107), Kant made much more of an impression with his philosophical works.

In *The Critique of Pure Reason* (1781), he produces a synthesis of the rationalism of Leibniz (see page 92), which holds that all knowledge is derived from deductions based on existing ideas, and the empiricism of Hume (see page 101), which holds that all knowledge is derived from observation alone. He concludes that we rely on the structure of our mind for our knowledge of the world, pure reason being something that can be known prior (*a priori*) to experience. In other words, the mind is no blank canvas passively waiting for objects to impinge upon it; instead, it plays an active part in acquiring knowledge by processing the information it perceives. And what we perceive in objects is the result of our make-up as an observer.

Kant felt his conclusions were the equivalent in philosophy of a Copernican revolution (Nicolas Copernicus discovering that the sun was the center of the universe). He identifies categories such as time and space, which don't exist externally and therefore can't be learned from experience; instead, they are the basic concepts of the framework that help us make sense of the world. Effectively, though the mind does not *create* the world, it does constitute the way the world appears.

For Kant, both the nature of reality and human morality are grounded in reason, which is the underlying principle of moral

> ⊙⊚ ⊙⊚ ⊙⊚
>
> **FOR KANT, BOTH THE NATURE OF REALITY AND HUMAN MORALITY ARE GROUNDED IN REASON, WHICH IS THE UNDERLYING PRINCIPLE OF MORAL PHILOSOPHY.**
>
> ⊙⊚ ⊙⊚ ⊙⊚

philosophy. Just as there is a law of nature, so there is a moral law, each of them the result of our mind imposing order on the welter of information received. In the *Groundwork of the Metaphysic of Morals* (1785), Kant refines his supreme moral law, the famous categorical imperative (see the quotation that starts this entry). Basically, if you want to do the right thing, adopt behavior that you would happily see applied as a universal principle, and which allows you to treat other people as ends in themselves, not merely as means to your ends.

The Critique of Practical Reason (1788) also deals with ethics and the search for moral laws, while *The Critique of Judgment* (1790) covers aesthetic judgments, which lead to theology: from art, via the artist conveying the beauties of nature, to the creator of that beautiful nature. As with his views on perception and

---

CONFUSED YET?

If not, try this from Kant's *Critique of Pure Reason*: "The assertorical speaks of logical reality or truth; as, for example, in a hypothetical syllogism, the antecedens presents itself in a problematical form in the major, in an assertorical form in the minor, and it shows that the proposition is in harmony with the laws of the understanding. The apodeictical proposition cogitates the assertorical as determined by these very laws of the understanding, consequently as affirming *a priori*, and in this manner it expresses logical necessity." Well, that's that sorted, then ...

ethics, Kant was seeking to establish an *a priori* principle of aesthetics to explain our comprehension of beauty.

Kant's philosophy, which he described as "transcendental" or "critical" idealism, attempted to reconcile the authority of science with people's everyday experience of a world bursting with moral, aesthetic, cultural and religious concerns.

INTO THE NINETEENTH CENTURY

The French Revolution and its aftereffects left Europe a legacy of political turmoil in the late eighteenth and early nineteenth centuries. The democratic ideals, the descent into bloodthirsty chaos and the Napoleonic Wars set in motion revolutionary rumblings at a time when advances in science and technology were empowering social groups not normally known for their political clout. Popular revolutions broke out in 1848—the date of Marx's *Communist Manifesto*—in France and Germany. While the workers of the world were being exhorted to unite, fired up by socialist, communist and anarchist ideas, their capitalist masters were espousing free-market liberalism. In the 1870s, maps had to be redrawn as nationalist movements in Germany and Italy saw the unification of those countries into the entities we recognize today. And behind all the political, social and economic upheavals, the philosophers were at work—sometimes producing theories that explained what they were witnessing, but occasionally seeming to create the impetus for action.

Jeremy Bentham

(1748–1832)

"...the greatest happiness of the greatest number
is the foundation of morals and legislation."

—*The Commonplace Book*

The son and grandson of lawyers, Jeremy Bentham was destined for a legal career. Born in London, he went to Oxford at the age of twelve and began his legal education when only fifteen. However, he soon decided that the law was too bound up in irrational technicalities and so made it his mission to clarify the foundations of a just and rational legal system.

The basis for Bentham's ideas, as laid out in his *Introduction to the Principles of Morals and Legislation* (1789), is utility: "that property in any object, whereby it tends to produce benefit, advantage, pleasure, good, or happiness...or...to prevent the happening of mischief, pain, evil, or unhappiness."

The way to judge if an action is right is by measuring its tendency to promote the greatest happiness for the greatest number, a philosophy known as utilitarianism. Happiness equals pleasure (including the absence of pain) and is achieved through the use of law and reason—the right law will produce happiness, the right law being the one that accords with reason, and thus with the principle of utility. To work out how likely an action is to promote happiness, Bentham devised a felicific or hedonistic ("happiness-inducing") calculus that took into account such things as the intensity, duration and likelihood of pleasures and pains.

Eager to put his ideas into practice, Bentham designed his famous prison, the Panopticon. This was a circular structure in

which the prisoners were incarcerated around a central observation tower, unable to tell whether they were being watched
at any given moment—or indeed whether there was anyone in
the tower at all—thereby being trained to monitor their own
behavior. Bentham believed that, since all punishment is pain,
it is only justified if it is outweighed by the reduction in pain
(or increase in pleasure) it causes in somebody else. So punishment is acceptable if people are deterred from doing things that
would lead to more pain, but there's no point in punishment for
punishment's sake.

For Bentham there weren't any such things as natural rights
or duties, or social contracts, either. The only rights were those

THE "AUTO-ICON"

Seated inside a wooden cabinet at University College London for all to see is the skeleton of Jeremy Bentham, wearing his own clothes, with a wax head (it should have been the real one, but something went horribly wrong with the preservation process). This is Bentham's "Auto-Icon," preserved for the benefit of posterity, according to the terms of Bentham's will.

based on law, linked with an authority to impose them on grounds of utility. Once people start talking about moral rights, they are appealing to a higher moral authority—which is irrational.

Bentham had hoped that politicians would see the advantage of introducing reforms to promote public happiness, but when they didn't, his enthusiasm for democratic reforms and wider voting rights grew. He thought that with educational improvements, more and more people would calculate rationally what was in their own long-term interest, leading to greater general happiness.

Georg Wilhelm Friedrich Hegel
(1770–1831)

"What is rational is real and what is real is rational."
—*The Philosophy of Right*

Born in Stuttgart, Georg Wilhelm Friedrich Hegel studied theology at Tübingen and worked as a tutor for some time before becoming a philosophy lecturer at Jena in 1801. Following Napoleon's victory at the Battle of Jena in 1806, however, the university was closed. The first of the four books published in Hegel's lifetime, *The Phenomenology of Spirit* (1807), appeared shortly afterward. During the nine years he then spent as a headmaster in Nuremberg, Hegel published his two-volume *Science of Logic* (1812 and 1816). In 1816 he became Professor of Philosophy at Heidelberg, where he wrote *The Encyclopedia of the Philosophical Sciences* (1817). His next appointment, in 1818, was as Professor of Philosophy in Berlin, and it was here that he wrote *The Philosophy of Right* (1821). He stayed in Berlin until

⊚⊚ ⊚⊚ ⊚⊚

**REALITY MUST BE
RATIONAL, HEGEL SAYS,
AND ITS FUNDAMENTAL
STRUCTURE IS MIRRORED
IN THE STRUCTURE OF OUR
THOUGHTS AS WE STRIVE TO
UNIFY WHAT AT FIRST SEEM
TO BE CONTRADICTIONS.**

⊚⊚ ⊚⊚ ⊚⊚

his death, during a cholera epidemic.

Considered by many the greatest of the German idealist philosophers (see Kant, page 106), Hegel constructed a comprehensive system of thought to make sense of what he saw around him. The world, he says, is not a collection of separate, contradictory units; despite appearances, these contradictory units are in fact all parts of the unified whole— the Absolute—since they can be combined, refined and developed to produce a more perfect comprehension of reality. Reality must be rational, and its fundamental structure is mirrored in the structure of our thoughts as we strive to unify what at first seem to be contradictions. The stages we go through to arrive at logical truths must be the same as the stages by which reality progresses. Key to this progression is Hegel's concept of "spirit," or mind, which by a dialectical process ultimately evolves into a higher form (see box, opposite).

In *The Phenomenology of Spirit* Hegel outlines the mind's development from basic consciousness, via self-consciousness and reason, to the pure consciousness of spirit, which is absolute knowledge. In *The Science of Logic* he explains how concepts of reality are revealed by dialectical reasoning: propose a thesis, consider its opposite or antithesis, and from the conflict between them a synthesis is born. This is the way in which human

HEGELIAN TRIADS

Nothing to do with Chinese gangsters, these triads are the three parts of Hegel's dialectical process. To use his example: first take your thesis, *being*; then come up with its antithesis, *nothing*; the resulting synthesis is becoming. Simple: thesis and antithesis are reconciled in the concept "becoming."

reasoning progresses; history, too, is moving in a similar way toward the Absolute, as his lecture notes (see below) make clear. In *The Encyclopedia of the Philosophical Sciences*, Hegel applies the dialectical approach to all areas of knowledge, while *The Philosophy of Right* contains his political philosophy.

Hegel's lecture notes on the philosophy of history—and also art, religion and philosophy—were published posthumously. He saw history as progress toward freedom: from the ancient empires of the East, where only rulers were free, via the Greeks with their devotion to the city-state, to the Protestant Reformation, when individuals realized they could achieve their own salvation. Hegel had enormous influence on German philosophy in the nineteenth century and, with his talk of historical progress, was central to the political theory of Karl Marx (see page 127), while his dialectical reasoning, minus the spirit, became Marx's dialectical materialism.

Arthur Schopenhauer
(1788–1860)

"Every man takes the limits of his own field
of vision for the limits of the world."

—*Studies in Pessimism*

Arthur Schopenhauer was born in Danzig (now Gdansk in Poland), the son of a successful merchant who was a great devotee of the works of Voltaire (see page 99), and a mother with literary aspirations. When Prussia annexed the city in 1793, the family moved to Hamburg. Schopenhauer was sent to school in France and England, after which he returned home and, to please his father, became a clerk. However, he hated the commercial life, seeing himself more as an academic, and when his father committed suicide in 1805, leaving him a substantial inheritance, he was free to rethink his future.

By 1809 Schopenhauer was studying philosophy at the university in Göttingen. In 1811 he moved to Berlin to pursue his studies and finally completed his dissertation in 1813 at Jena. Entitled "On the Fourfold Root of the Principle of Sufficient Reason," it challenged the idea that what is real is what is rational—or, in other words, that the world is knowable; when his mother declared it unreadable, that was the end of their relationship. In 1814, Schopenhauer moved to Dresden, where he began work on his most famous book, *The World as Will and Representation* (1818). He became a lecturer at Berlin University in 1820 but had the temerity to schedule his lectures to coincide with those of Hegel (see page 115), whose work he despised. Since Hegel was the professor, Schopenhauer failed to attract many students, took umbrage and gave up his academic career to devote himself to writing.

For Schopenhauer, a declared atheist, the world is nothing but a series of momentary impressions, while the ultimate reality is the will—aimless, irrational, impenetrable and implacable. One of the first philosophers to be influenced by Eastern ideas—both Hindu and Buddhist—Schopenhauer insisted on the universality of suffering and held that salvation could be achieved only by overcoming the will through asceticism and renunciation. He identified three ways forward: studying philosophy; contemplating works of art and listening to music; and having compassion for others. Among his later works, *On the Will in Nature* (1836) claims backing for his ideas from the empirical sciences, while *On the Basis of Morality* (1840) tackles such issues as freedom and determinism. In 1844 he published a revised edition of *The World as Will and Representation* with fifty additional chapters, thus almost doubling the size of the first edition, but it still did not make a big impression. It was only with the publication of *Parerga and Paralipomena* (1851), a late collection of philosophical essays and insights, that he finally received the attention he felt he deserved.

Though he tends to be billed as a confirmed pessimist, Schopenhauer did suggest ways, especially through art, to transcend the frustrations of the human condition. For that reason his ideas have appealed to

@@ @@ @@

SCHOPENHAUER IDENTIFIED THREE WAYS FORWARD: STUDYING PHILOSOPHY; CONTEMPLATING WORKS OF ART AND LISTENING TO MUSIC; AND HAVING COMPASSION FOR OTHERS.

@@ @@ @@

numerous writers and musicians, such as Thomas Mann, Proust, Tolstoy and Wagner, as well as other philosophers, including Nietzsche (see page 130).

DO AS I SAY....

Although Schopenhauer declared that compassion was the main drive toward ethical behavior, he doesn't seem to have been very driven in that direction himself. He was found guilty of kicking a seamstress down a flight of stairs and had to pay her a regular allowance in compensation. On her death he uttered the Latin words, *"Obit anus, abit onus"*—"The old woman dies, the burden goes away."

It is with trifles, and when he is off guard, that a man best reveals his character.

John Stuart Mill

(1806–73)

"Bad men need nothing more to compass their ends,
than that good men should look on and do nothing."
—Inaugural address delivered at
St. Andrews University, 1867

Born in London, the son of the Scottish philosopher and historian James Mill, John Stuart Mill was a gifted child who was rigorously trained for greatness by his father. He studied Greek from the age of three; Latin came later, when he was all of eight, followed by logic and political economy in his early teens, and then history, law and philosophy. The idea was to equip the younger Mill to join the ranks of the Philosophical Radicals and champion the Benthamite cause (see box on page 122). For a while John Stuart Mill did as his father wished, helping to form the Utilitarian Society and contributing to the *Westminster Review*. In 1826, however, he had what he later referred to as a "mental crisis" and from that time on became less of a hard-line utilitarian proselytizer.

Mill was a committed empiricist, convinced that truths could be obtained only from experience. He felt that the alternative—relying on intuition—simply reinforced existing prejudices. His first major work, the one that established his reputation as England's pre-eminent nineteenth-century philosopher, was *A System of Logic* (1843). The book details the principles of logic and mathematics, then discusses deduction and induction, observation and classification, fallacies of reasoning and the moral sciences. There was a clear practical dimension to all this, as Mill hoped his system would help to bring about social and political change.

The book for which he is best known, *On Liberty* (1859), discusses the freedom of the individual in relation to society and the state, arguing that "the only purpose for which power can be rightfully exercised over any member of a civilized community, against his will, is to prevent harm to others. His own good, either physical or moral, is not a sufficient warrant." Mill's position was not premised on ideas of rights but on a belief in utility: if everyone pursued their own happiness, together they would further the general good of society. The majority should not force out those who disagree with them and free speech should be encouraged, because genuine debate allows people to examine their convictions.

Utilitarianism (1863) proposes that there are objective standards of right and good, with good equating to the greatest happiness. Adding a twist on Jeremy Bentham, though, Mill distinguishes between higher and lower pleasures. *The Subjection*

THE PHILOSOPHICAL RADICALS

The name says it all: this was a group of radical thinkers inspired by the utilitarian philosophy of Jeremy Bentham (see page 112) and James Mill. Several, including John Stuart Mill, the latter's son, became Members of Parliament, where they used their influence to advocate political reform. The group's mouthpiece was the *Westminster Review*, a quarterly founded by Bentham and James Mill in 1823.

of Women (1869) develops his arguments for the freedom of the individual.

For thirty-five years, until it folded in 1858, John Stuart Mill worked for the East India Company, as his father had done before him. In 1865 he entered Parliament, where he was a strong advocate of women's rights, among other liberal concerns, such as trade unionism and the abolition of slavery. Interestingly, he was the godfather of Bertrand Russell (see page 134).

Søren Kierkegaard
(1813–55)

"… knowledge has a relationship to the knower,
who is essentially an existing individual, and [that]
for this reason all essential knowledge is essentially
related to existence."

—*Concluding Unscientific Postscript to Philosophical Fragments*

Credited as the father of existentialism (see page 150), Søren Kierkegaard was born into an affluent family in Copenhagen. The youngest of seven children, he was brought up in a household dominated by his deeply religious and melancholic father, Michael, who believed he had been cursed by God as a child—he feared that none of his offspring would survive him and was right about five of them. Kierkegaard studied theology at the university in Copenhagen but found himself increasingly drawn to philosophy and literature. Trying to be practical, he planned to become a cleric and to marry, but then in 1840 broke off his engagement and abandoned all thoughts of a

Church career. Instead, he would be an author. Over the next ten years he wrote numerous books and pamphlets, including several major philosophical works. He often adopted pseudonyms, not to conceal his identity but to allow him to take different viewpoints.

Kierkegaard positioned himself firmly against the dominant German traditions of the day, in particular Hegel's contention that life could be explained by intellect alone. He saw this as a misguided attempt to replace God by elevating man, despite all the limitations on man's ability to make objective judgements. Instead, he focused on the importance of the individual, stressing the centrality of the will and of free choice. For Kierkegaard, where human action and judgment were concerned, subjectivity was all. He carried his philosophical approach over into his works against organized Christianity, which he referred to disparag-

---

ANGST

The English-speaking world has Kierkegaard to thank for introducing this word to describe the sense of profound insecurity and fear that haunts human beings. In Danish *angst* means "anxiety" or "dread," and it was used by Kierkegaard in his book *The Concept of Anxiety* (1844) — also known as *The Concept of Dread*, depending on the translator. Kierkegaard believed that freedom of choice leaves people in a state of perpetual anxiety about their responsibilities to God. For later existentialists it was more a case of responsibilities to oneself, one's principles and other people.

ingly as Christendom. Here he again stressed individual choice as opposed to blind acceptance of the rituals of the Danish Lutheran Church.

In *Either/Or* (1843), Kierkegaard contrasts the aesthetic and the ethical ways of life. The former revolves around immediate pleasure—whether sensory,

◎◎ ◎◎ ◎◎

KIERKEGAARD FOCUSED ON THE IMPORTANCE OF THE INDIVIDUAL, STRESSING THE CENTRALITY OF THE WILL AND OF FREE CHOICE.

◎◎ ◎◎ ◎◎

physical or intellectual—while the latter is grounded in morality and the hereafter. Once people understand that the aesthetic path leads only to anxiety and despair, they will, he says, opt for the ethical. In *Fear and Trembling* (1843) he explains that, because God is essentially unknowable, a leap of faith is necessary to move on from the ethical to the religious way, citing as an example Abraham's acceptance of God's order to sacrifice his beloved son Isaac. This "teleological suspension of the ethical" demonstrates the ultimate in religious conviction and unconditional obedience to God's will. Kierkegaard was on a one-man mission to "reintroduce Christianity into Christendom."

It is in *Philosophical Fragments* (1844) and *Concluding Unscientific Postscripts to Philosophical Fragments* (1846) that Kierkegaard spells out his challenge to the Hegelian notion of a "science of the spirit." For him "subjectivity is truth," in contrast with Hegel's "what is rational is real."

Kierkegaard's works exerted great influence on those concerned with problems of religion and ethics, especially the existentialists among them.

A PRAGMATIC DUO

The word "pragmatism" was introduced into philosophy by the American Charles Peirce (1839–1914), who formulated his pragmatic maxim to clarify the meaning of any given concept: "We must look to the upshot of our concepts in order rightly to apprehend them." So pragmatism was not so much a philosophical system as a theory of meaning.

A scientist by training, Peirce believed that concepts need to be tested in the way that scientific hypotheses are. Just as we analyze scientific ideas by looking at the effects they have and the way we can make use of them, so the truth of a theory is inseparable from its consequences. And once we've all agreed that something is true, it becomes our reality. He felt obliged to coin the word pragmaticism for his own distinctive approach once his compatriot William James (1842–1910), brother of the novelist Henry James, started to expand pragmatism's application beyond Peirce's theory of meaning.

James, a graduate of Harvard Medical School and author of *Principles of Psychology* (1890), which is credited with laying the foundations of the subject as it is studied to this day, took Peirce's ideas further. James argued that if a concept means literally what you do with it, then its truth must consist in doing whatever it is successfully. Ideas, just like minds, he was sure, can be studied by their function. In *Pragmatism* (1907), his best-known philosophical work, James states that concepts are part of an active process, not just static things to be examined. He turned meaning into action.

Karl Marx

(1818–83)

"The philosophers have only interpreted the world in
various ways. The point however is to change it."
—"Eleventh Thesis on Feuerbach" and on Marx's
tombstone in Highgate Cemetery, London

Karl Marx was born and brought up in Trier, a cosmopolitan
Prussian city, by parents who had converted from Judaism to
avoid anti-Semitism. Having studied law at Bonn for a year, in
1836 he moved to Berlin, where his interest in philosophy developed under the influence of the Young Hegelians, a group that
opposed the idealist teachings of Hegel in favor of materialism
but made use of Hegel's dialectical method (see below).

In 1842 Marx started editing the liberal Cologne-based
Rheinische Zeitung, but it was suppressed by the government
the following year, and he moved to Paris. Here he became a
communist and met Friedrich Engels, who was to be a lifelong
friend. Marx left France for political reasons in 1845 and went to
Brussels, where he collaborated with Engels on *German Ideology*
(1845–6), which introduced Marx's "materialist conception of
history," and the famous *Communist Manifesto* (1848). In 1848,
after a brief stint back in Paris, he returned to Cologne to edit
the *Neue Rheinische Zeitung*, a more radical version of his old
paper. When that, too, was closed down in 1849, he moved to
London, where he lived for the rest of his life.

In the reading room of the British Museum, Marx began
work on *Capital* (1867), one of the most influential books of all

time. It contains his definitive views on the theory of surplus value (profits made by capitalists) and the exploitation of the working classes, and anticipates the overthrow of capitalism by socialism and the emergence of a classless communist society. The philosophical underpinnings of these ideas were historical and dialectical materialism.

If eighteenth-century materialism is the doctrine that nothing exists except matter, historical materialism is Marx's new take: the application of dialectical methods to historical evolution, showing among other things that humans have, through the ages, entered into—and been defined by—social contracts designed to maintain production of the necessities of life. A division of labor coupled with a division of society into classes—whether slaves and masters or workers and capitalists—is historically how humans have organized and sustained themselves.

The ideas first outlined in *German Ideology*—humans are different from other animals because they produce what they need to survive; what they are depends on how and what they produce; their nature is conditioned by their material conditions—were expanded in *Contribution to the Critique of Political Economy* (1859): "It is not the consciousness of men that determines their existence, but, on the contrary, their social existence that determines their consciousness."

Which leads to dialectical materialism. Marx contrasts

> ◎◎ ◎◎ ◎◎
>
> AS MARX SAW IT, EACH STAGE OF SOCIETY GENERATED FORCES THAT WOULD BRING IT DOWN, WITH A NEW SOCIETY EMERGING FROM THE CONFLICT: THESIS/ANTI-THESIS/SYNTHESIS.
>
> ◎◎ ◎◎ ◎◎

his dialectic method to Hegel's: "To Hegel...the process of thinking, which, under the name of 'the Idea,' he even transforms into an independent subject, is the demiurgos of the real world, and the real world is only the external, phenomenal form of 'the Idea.' With me...the ideal is nothing else than the material world reflected by the human mind, and translated into forms of thought."

As Marx saw it, each stage of society generated forces that would bring it down, with a new society emerging from the conflict: thesis/antithesis/synthesis.

Marx took philosophy out into the real world, with all its political and economic complexities. Though many of his doctrines had terrible practical consequences—think Stalin's Russia, Mao's China—the idea that the economy prompts historical change is still influential.

Friedrich Nietzsche

(1844–1900)

"What I understand by 'philosopher': a terrible explosive in the presence of which everything is in danger."

—*Ecce Homo*

Born in the province of Saxony, the son of a Lutheran pastor, Nietzsche was a brilliant student during his time at the universities of Bonn and Leipzig. At Bonn he studied theology and philology, with a view to becoming a pastor, too, but once he lost his faith, that route was closed to him. He moved to Leipzig to concentrate on philology, and it was here that he came across a copy of Schopenhauer's *The World as Will and Representation* (see page 118). He became Professor of Philology at the University of Basel in 1869, at only twenty-four. For a short time in 1870, he was a medical orderly in the Franco-Prussian War, from which he returned in bad health. This was the start of a long decline, both physical and mental, that forced him to resign from the university in 1878 and left him insane from 1889 until his death.

Nietzsche wasn't the conventional sort of philosopher, laboring methodically to construct a new theory about the nature of knowledge. Instead, he ranged widely over questions of morality and religion in a number of intensely written works that ponder what makes human beings act they way they do.

In his first book, *The Birth of Tragedy* (1872), Nietzsche compares "Apollonian" and "Dionysian" values in ancient Greece—order and reason vs. primal instincts—concerned that the importance of the latter has been overlooked and seeing much to admire in the heroic qualities of Homer's warriors.

Essays and books of aphorisms followed, in which Nietzsche identifies fear and the striving for power as key motivators: the "will to power," he goes on to claim, is the fundamental human drive. In *Thus Spoke Zarathustra* (1883) and *Beyond Good and Evil* (1886), he proposes a new life-affirming morality based on confident self-assertion. The will to power is embodied in his *Übermensch* ("superman"), who is strong enough to break free from conventional morality, control his passions and direct his energies toward creativity: this is "master-morality." Rather than wait for an imaginary afterlife, the superman lives fully in the here and now.

THE WILL TO POWER IS EMBODIED IN NIETZSCHE'S *ÜBERMENSCH* ("SUPERMAN"), WHO IS STRONG ENOUGH TO BREAK FREE FROM CONVENTIONAL MORALITY, CONTROL HIS PASSIONS AND DIRECT HIS ENERGIES TOWARD CREATIVITY: THIS IS "MASTER-MORALITY."

The will to power went hand in hand with Nietzsche's virulent opposition to Christianity, which he believed was nothing but a denial of the life-affirming passions. Christianity promoted the weak and the downtrodden, encouraging a "slave-morality"that had no place in his brave new world. For Nietzsche developments in science and secular reasoning had undermined religion—indeed, killed it off: "God is dead," he announced. Now that the universal perspective given by God had gone, people would follow their own values, with ethics grounded in human existence rather than divine revelation.

Nietzsche feared that Europe would sink into nihilism without a new morality. He rejected democracy, "bourgeois" values and utilitarian ethics—more slave stuff. Happiness and "the greater good" were feeble goals, lacking the life-affirming qualities of the masters: power, wealth, strength and health—all things Nietzsche was lacking by the end of his life. And it did his reputation no good at all when the Nazis absorbed his "super-man" into their ideology of a master race.

MODERN TIMES

All that budding European nationalism in the nineteenth century was bound to end in tears. The First World War swept away the certainties of the Victorian era, and the political fallout significantly altered the map of Europe. The economic consequences in both America and Europe followed a path of boom and bust that's oh so familiar today, while also contributing to the outbreak of the Second World War, with all the horrors that entailed.

In the philosophical world another war was declared, as the lines were drawn between the Anglo-American (or analytical) school and the Continentals. In the former camp were philosophers such as Russell, Moore and Wittgenstein, who relied on mathematical logic and linguistic analysis to isolate and then deal with discrete philosophical questions. Opposing them were the likes of Heidegger, Sartre, Foucault and Derrida, who saw philosophy as inseparable from its historical background, developing their theories of existentialism, structuralism and post-structuralism, which seemed like so much obfuscation to the analytical establishment.

Bertrand Russell

(1872–1970)

"Mathematics, rightly viewed, possesses not only truth,
but supreme beauty—a beauty cold and austere,
like that of sculpture."

— in his essay "The Study of Mathematics"

Born in Monmouthshire (now Wales) into an aristocratic family, Bertrand Russell was orphaned by the age of four and brought up by his grandmother. He was educated at home, studying modern languages, economics, constitutional history, mathematics and science—rather than Greek and Latin, as would have been more usual for someone of his background—and this laid the foundations for his wide-ranging intellectual interests. In 1890 he went to Cambridge to study mathematics, switching to philosophy in 1893 and graduating with first-class honors the following year. He became a fellow in 1895, shortly after getting married. On returning from his honeymoon in Berlin, Russell wrote *German Social Democracy* (1896). Around the same time, he encountered the work of a group of German mathematicians who, by analyzing the fundamental concepts of mathematics, were trying to provide it with logically coherent foundations. For Russell their ideas had significance not only for mathematics but also for philosophy: if mathematical truth could be proved objectively, why not the truth about human knowledge, too?

Rejecting the Hegelian idealist philosophy that he had so far espoused, with its quest for overarching systems (see page 115), Russell focused instead on in-depth logical analysis. In *Principles of Mathematics* (1903) he argued that math should be treated as a subset of logic, while the three-volume *Principia Mathematica* (1910–13), which he wrote with Alfred North Whitehead, reinforced the idea of the logical derivation of mathematics, with additional philosophical analysis that demonstrated how everyday language and grammar were not always clear enough to convey true logical forms. This built on an earlier essay, "On Denoting" (1905), in which Russell highlighted the philosophical problems raised by the slipperiness of language in relation to naming and describing objects: how was it possible to speak meaningfully of non-existent things or even things that can't possibly exist?

His answer was to keep things as simple as possible by subjecting the meaning of words and how they are used to the same sort of rigorous analysis that would be used on mathematical concepts. This analytical approach—Russell was one of the founders of analytic philosophy—led away from the search for grand metaphysical systems toward the study of linguistics and logical positivism, not to mention atomism (see page 40).

Russell was renowned for his ability to convey complex ideas to a general audience, with fast-selling books on such subjects as science, politics, ethics and educational theory, plus mathematics and philosophy. His *History of Western Philosophy* appeared in 1945 and has been in print ever since.

In 1950 Russell was awarded the Nobel Prize for Literature.

G. E. Moore

(1873–1958)

"All moral laws…are merely statements that certain
kinds of actions will have good effects."

—*Principia Ethica*

Born in London, G. E. Moore was educated at Dulwich College and then Cambridge. He was originally studying classics, but once he became friendly with Bertrand Russell (see page 134), he switched to philosophy. After graduating, Moore spent some time studying on his own before returning to Cambridge in 1911 to lecture in philosophy. He was Professor of Mental Philosophy and Logic from 1925 to 1939,

BLOOMSBURY CONNECTIONS

While at Cambridge, Russell and Moore joined the select discussion group the Cambridge Apostles. Among other Apostles were Roger Fry, John Maynard Keynes, E. M. Forster and Lytton Strachey, all of whom were to play a major role in the Bloomsbury Group.

That much-biographied happy band, which included Clive and Vanessa Bell and Virginia Woolf, met regularly from around 1905 to 1930 in Bloomsbury, central London. Fry became best known as an art critic, Keynes as an economist, Forster a novelist and Strachey a biographer and critic. Their discussions on aesthetic and philosophical issues, not to mention their behavior, were heavily influenced by Moore's *Principia Ethica* (1903) and Whitehead and Russell's *Principia Mathematica* (1910–13), which led them to come up with their own definitions of the good, the true and the beautiful, challenging the artistic, social and sexual restrictions of Victorian society.

at which point he was succeeded by Ludwig Wittgenstein (see page 141). He also edited the influential philosophy journal *Mind* from 1921 to 1944.

As he wrote in the autobiographical *Philosophy of G. E. Moore* (1942), Moore was puzzled in his early career not so much by the world or the sciences, but by the things other philosophers had said about them. Like Russell, he found he could not sustain his initial fascination with Hegelian idealism (see page 115), so he moved toward a simpler, more analytical approach. This he expounded first in his article, "The Refutation of Idealism," which appeared in *Mind* in 1903, and then in later works such as *A Defense of Common Sense* (1925) and *Proof of an External World* (1939). He started from the position that no sensible person could disagree that a large body of shared beliefs about the world existed and that these could be expressed as straightforward propositions, the meanings of which were not only perfectly clear but also palpably true.

All of which meant, Moore felt, that earlier philosophers must have been mistaken either about the nature of philosophy or in their approach toward it. Why did they agonize over problems of meaning, when there were none, or over the truth of propositions, as that was beyond doubt, too? According to Moore, this left just one thing for philosophers to do: analyze these straightforward propositions to extract their significance.

His *Principia Ethica* (1903) considers what's known as the naturalistic fallacy—the confusion between natural attribution and moral definition—with a view to analyzing the fundamental moral question "What is goodness?" You cannot, Moore says, define "good" in terms of, say, happiness, because that just raises another question: "Is happiness always good?" Other properties can be attributed to "good," but they too only illustrate it rather than define it. Moore concludes that goodness is a simple, unanalyzable

@@ @@ @@

MOORE WAS PUZZLED IN HIS EARLY CAREER NOT SO MUCH BY THE WORLD OR THE SCIENCES, BUT BY THE THINGS OTHER PHILOSOPHERS HAD SAID ABOUT THEM.

@@ @@ @@

quality, known simply by intuition. The best we can do is to ask what *things* are good, and here he had no hesitation in providing the answer: friendship and aesthetic experience. No wonder he was so popular with the Bloomsbury Group (see box on page 137).

Martin Heidegger
(1889–1976)

"The most thought-provoking thing in our thought-provoking time is that we are still not thinking."
— *What is Called Thinking?*

Born in Messkirch, Germany, the son of a Catholic sexton, Martin Heidegger joined the Jesuits as a novice after leaving school but abandoned the idea a month later. Instead, he went to Freiburg University to study theology, switching later to philosophy. He started lecturing in philosophy there in 1915, was appointed professor at Marburg in 1923 and then returned to Freiburg as professor in 1928. He became rector in 1933, joining the Nazi Party shortly afterward, and in his inaugural address, "The Role of the University in the New Reich," expressed support for Hitler and his aims—which is the first thing people tend to remember about Heidegger today.

His most important work, the unfinished—and some would say unfinishable—*Being and Time* (1927), introduces the topic that resonates through much of his later writings: the "question of being" (*Seinsfrage*). Rather than simply take for granted what it means for someone to "be," Heidegger felt it was necessary to question the metaphysical models used by earlier philosophers from Aristotle onward. As far as he could see, metaphysics does not reveal anything about the true nature of being; instead, all that really exists is people's consciousness of their own place in the world, or of what the world means to them (their "being-there" or *Dasein*). This then brings in the time angle of the book's title. Because life is finite, humans must remain constantly aware of the inevitability of their own death in order to live authentically. They are free to choose their actions and focus their energies within the world they have been born into: the possibilities do not stop until death.

Heidegger was troubled by the sense that modern technology was divorcing people from what he called the "nearness and shelter" of being, making life "inauthentic" in a way that had not been true for their more primitive ancestors, who had lived in happy communion with nature.

All of this opens the way to some of the major themes of twentieth-century history and thought: individual freedom, one's place in the world, authenticity, angst, guilt and destiny. The Second World War was on the horizon, while such existentialists as Jean-Paul Sartre (see page 149) and deconstructionists as Jacques Derrida (see page 157) were waiting in the wings.

Ludwig Wittgenstein
(1889–1951)

"Whereof one cannot speak, thereof one
must be silent."

—*Tractatus Logico-Philosophicus*

The youngest of eight children, Ludwig Wittgenstein was born in Vienna into a wealthy and cultured family. His father was a hugely successful industrialist, a great music lover and an art collector; Wittgenstein was intended to be the practical member of the family. From 1906 to 1908, he studied mechanical engineering in Berlin. He then went to Manchester University, where he became fascinated by mathematics, so in 1911 he moved to Cambridge to study mathematical logic with Bertrand Russell (see page 134). After two years Russell declared that he had taught Wittgenstein all he could. While Russell's interest was uncovering the logical foundations of mathematics, Wittgenstein wanted to fathom the foundations of logic itself. At the start of the First World War, he joined the Austrian army, but for the next four years he worked on what was to become *Tractatus Logico-Philosophicus* (1922), the only book published in his lifetime.

In a preface written in 1918, Wittgenstein boldly declared, "I therefore believe myself to have found, on all essential points, the final solution of the problems"—as in the problems of philoso-

---

THE VIENNA CIRCLE

This group of academics at Vienna University in the 1920s and 1930s were known as logical positivists—or logical empiricists—because their interest in the sciences and mathematics led them to identify mathematical logic as the way to handle philosophical problems.

Wittgenstein's *Tractatus Logico-Philosophicus* was of enormous influence, although he did not join the group. In 1929, they produced a pamphlet outlining their basic tenets: knowledge comes from experience (the positivist/empiricist bit) and philosophical problems must be clarified before they can be tackled (that's logical), with propositions that can't be verified dismissed as meaningless (no more discussions of ethics, religion and aesthetics). Their influence soon spread beyond the German-speaking world, but within a few years the group had dispersed because of Nazi hostility and the onset of the war.

phy. It was all a question of language—specifically, its nature and limitations.

The world is made up of discrete "atomic" facts, from which larger facts can be built. Language, the purpose of which is to state the facts, is similarly made up of "atomic" propositions, from which larger propositions can

@@ @@ @@

WITTGENSTEIN SEES LANGUAGE AS A MEANS OF COMMUNICATING AND FURTHERING SOCIAL FUNCTIONS IN THE REAL WORLD, AND THEREFORE SOMETHING THAT CHANGES ACCORDING TO CONTEXT.

@@ @@ @@

be built. Language and thought together create a picture of the state of affairs to which they refer. To be meaningful, language must comprise propositions that are pictures of the facts the world is composed of; it must refer to the real. Which makes a great deal of speculative philosophy, not to mention value judgments, literally meaningless. And if the limits of language are also the limits of thought...well, see the quotation at the start of this entry. Having devised this logically coherent scheme, thanks to which no one need ever talk nonsense again, Wittgenstein felt he'd reached the end of the line with philosophy and started to look for a new career. But it turned out that this was just the end of philosophy phase one.

Wittgenstein had inherited a fortune when his father died in 1913, and he now gave it away, opting from 1920 for the life of a schoolteacher in rural Austria instead. When this experiment failed, he turned his hand to architecture, building a house for one of his sisters in Vienna. While there, in 1929, he met members of the Vienna Circle (see box, opposite), who were busy developing the ideas of the *Tractatus* into the rigorous tenets of logical positivism. Their activities must have persuaded Wittgenstein that philosophy still held more challenges, because he returned to Cambridge that year, first as a fellow of Trinity College and then, from 1939 to 1947, as Professor of Philosophy. Here his work took a new turn, summarized in *Philosophical Investigations* (1953), which seems to reject most of what was said in the *Tractatus*.

In this later work Wittgenstein no longer sees language as a static, logical system; it is now a means of communicating and furthering social functions in the real world, and therefore something that changes according to context. He identifies what he calls "language games"—different sorts of language with different uses—that each have their own rules but come together to make up a toolkit for philosophers. Clarity can only come by acknowledging this diversity. For Wittgenstein, by the end, the aim seems to be to use language to untangle the linguistic tangles philosophers have made, thus doing away with problems rather than needing to solve them.

Gilbert Ryle
(1900–1976)

"...the dogma of the ghost in the machine
[referring to Cartesian dualism]."
—*The Concept of Mind*

Born in Brighton, England, Gilbert Ryle studied at Oxford and started lecturing in philosophy there in 1924. Having worked in intelligence during the Second World War, he returned to

Oxford in 1945 to become Professor of Metaphysical Philosophy, a position he held until his retirement in 1968. From 1947 until 1971, following in the footsteps of G. E. Moore (see page 136), he was also the editor of *Mind*.

An advocate of linguistic analysis, or the "ordinary

◎◎ ◎◎ ◎◎

RYLE FELT THAT HIS JOB AS A PHILOSOPHER WAS TO ROOT OUT "THE SOURCES IN LINGUISTIC IDIOMS OF RECURRENT MISCONCEPTIONS AND ABSURD THEORIES."

◎◎ ◎◎ ◎◎

language" school of philosophy, Ryle felt that his job as a philosopher was to root out "the sources in linguistic idioms of recurrent misconceptions and absurd theories." As far as he could see, errors and confusion in philosophy came about when expressions that clearly belonged to one logical category were treated as if they belonged to another: what he refers to as category mistakes. The example often cited is taken from his major work, *The Concept of Mind* (1949): "She came home in a flood of tears and a sedan-chair." Though this is a perfectly well-turned sentence from a syntactical point of view, it is also absurd in that it is treating a state of mind and a material object as if they were one and the same. Ryle's idea is that, by pushing expressions to the limits of absurdity in this way, philosophical problems can be exposed and dealt with.

This is the method he uses in the same book to dismantle what he calls the "official doctrine" of philosophy: Cartesian dualism (see page 87)—the separation of mind and body. For Ryle this was the category mistake to end all category mistakes, and it stemmed from the fact that Descartes did not have our knowledge of biology. Ryle can see no logical reason for treating the mind as some sort of ghostly entity to be tacked on to the human body, which is acknowledged to exist in space and is subject to physical laws. Rather, mental concepts such as emotions, sensations, self-knowledge, imagination and the intellect should be seen as innate human dispositions that behave in certain ways in certain circumstances—in other words, there is no split between mind and body.

Throughout his career Ryle wrote widely not just on the philosophy of language but also on epistemology (the study of knowledge) and the history of philosophy, and it was his influence that helped make Oxford a center of philosophical study after the war.

Karl Popper
(1902–94)

"…it is very hard to learn from very big mistakes."
—*The Open Society and Its Enemies*

Karl Popper was born into an affluent family in Vienna, capital of the Austro-Hungarian Empire, and went to the university there in 1918. He briefly became a Marxist, but resisted the mental straitjacket he felt historical materialism imposed. By the time he graduated in 1922, the empire had been dismembered in the wake of the First World War and his family had lost all their money. However, Vienna remained an intellectual center, home to the psychiatrists Sigmund Freud and Alfred Adler, as well as the logical positivists of the Vienna Circle (see box on page 142), whose interest in the natural sciences Popper shared.

WITTGENSTEIN'S POKER

In 1946 Karl Popper delivered a lecture to the Cambridge University Moral Science Club entitled "Are There Philosophical Problems?" His contention that there were incensed at least one listener, Ludwig Wittgenstein (see page 141), who believed that philosophy had no right to concern itself with such issues, being all a question of language. For ten minutes their tussle was purely verbal, until Wittgenstein picked up a poker and started waving it around. In Popper's version of events, the confrontation ended when Wittgenstein asked for an example of a moral rule and Popper came up with, "Not to threaten visiting lecturers with pokers"—at which point Wittgenstein dropped the offending object and stalked off. Of course, this is just Popper's version....

He worked as a schoolteacher from 1930 but immigrated to New Zealand in 1937, worried by the prospect of German occupation. He lectured in philosophy at Canterbury University College until 1945, when he moved to the London School of Economics. There he was Professor of Logic and Scientific Method from 1949 until 1969.

Popper's main interests were the philosophy of science and political philosophy. Though he was associated with the Vienna Circle, his early work argues that philosophical problems can't be tackled through an analysis of language or meaning; nor does he consider science more verifiable than metaphysics. In *The Logic of Scientific Discovery* (1934), he challenges the idea that science is a process of induction, with theories coming from repeated observations and proved by experiment. Further, he claims that it's actually impossible to verify a scientific theory since no amount of observation can show beyond doubt that a hypothesis is true, while only one observation is needed to refute it. Which makes falsification the way to go.

Popper distinguishes between science, which generates theories leading to empirical predictions that can be jettisoned when the experiment fails, and non-science. The theories of Freud, Adler and Marx fall into the latter camp, as psychiatry cannot generate empirical predictions and Marxism is never knocked off course by observational disproof. It is with true science—the theories of Einstein, say—that hypotheses can be proved wrong if a single observation goes against them. Eliminating falsified theories leaves only objective scientific knowledge, which corresponds to the truth.

As for Popper's political philosophy, in *The Open Society and Its Enemies* (1945) and *The Poverty of Historicism* (1957) he disputes the idea that history has inevitable outcomes, seeing this as simply another untestable, unscientific assertion to justify the actions of fanatics and oppressors—he challenges the views of Plato, Hegel and Marx (see pages 32, 115 and 127) in this respect. History, he says, will always be affected by future discoveries that no one can possibly know about, and political actions, however well intentioned, will always have unforeseen consequences. So, instead, he makes a heartfelt plea for open, democratic societies that allow gentle "social engineering" when necessary.

Jean-Paul Sartre
(1905–80)

"Man, being condemned to be free, carries the weight
of the whole world on his shoulders; he is responsible
for the world and for himself as a way of being."
—*Being and Nothingness*

Born and educated in Paris, where he attended the prestigious Ecole Normale Supérieure—as Foucault and Derrida (see pages 154 and 157) would also do—Jean-Paul Sartre started teaching philosophy in Le Havre in 1931. Having been awarded a grant to study at the French Institute in Berlin, he spent 1934 and 1935 pursuing his interest in the work of contemporary German philosophers, especially Heidegger (see page 139). When he returned to France, Sartre taught in Le Havre, Laon and Paris, and also published his first novel, *Nausea* (1938). Conscripted at the outbreak of the Second World War, he was captured by the Germans in June 1940 and sent to a prisoner-of-war camp, where he ran classes for fellow inmates on the work of Heidegger.

Following his release in spring 1941, he taught in Paris for the rest of the war and was also active in the French Resistance. Once hostilities were over, he abandoned academia in favor of writing for a wider audience and active political engagement.

Sartre is synonymous with existentialism, the principles of which he defined in his philosophical writings, embodied in his plays and novels, and lived out to the end of his life. As he states in his 1946 lecture "Existentialism is a Humanism": "Atheistic existentialism, of which I am a representative, declares...that if God does not exist there is at least one being whose existence comes before its essence, a being which exists before it can be defined by any conception of it. That being is man or, as Heidegger has it, the human reality. What do we mean by saying that existence precedes essence? We mean that man first of all exists, encounters himself, surges up in the world—and defines himself afterward. If man as the existentialist sees him is not definable, it is because to begin with he is nothing. He will not be anything until later, and then he will be what he makes of himself. Thus, there is no human nature, because there is no God to have a conception of it. Man simply is.... That is the first principle of existentialism."

In the earlier *Being and Nothingness* (1943), Sartre had already explored the problem at the heart of existentialism: if we are all ultimately alone, each of us responsible

❦❦ ❦❦ ❦❦

SARTRE IS SYNONYMOUS WITH EXISTENTIALISM, THE PRINCIPLES OF WHICH HE DEFINED IN HIS PHILOSOPH-ICAL WRITINGS, EMBODIED IN HIS PLAYS AND NOVELS, AND LIVED OUT TO THE END OF HIS LIFE.

❦❦ ❦❦ ❦❦

for what we make of ourselves—"condemned to be free"—how can we relate to other people and things in the world? He saw two options. Either we passively accept the status quo, operating as mere objects, or we challenge the current situation and aspire to something better. But that just leads to another question: in a world in which we have no allegiance except to ourselves, how is moral action or political commitment possible?

Sartre attempts to provide answers through plays such as *No Exit* (1944) and novels such as the *Roads to Freedom* trilogy (1945–9). As he made clear in *What is Literature?* (1947), he saw writing as a way to tackle issues relating to human freedom. Literature must be committed, since artistic creation is a moral activity. This means writers have a duty to participate in social and political issues, which explains Sartre's involvement with Marxism and then the radical New Left in France.

A. J. Ayer
(1910–89)

"The criterion which we use to test the genuineness
of apparent statements of fact is the
criterion of verifiability."

—*Language, Truth and Logic*

Born in London and educated at Eton and Oxford, Alfred Jules Ayer was a pupil of Gilbert Ryle (see page 144). He worked in intelligence during the Second World War and then, in 1946, after a period in Paris as attaché at the British embassy,

A. J. AYER KNOCKS OUT MIKE TYSON

In 1982 the philosopher attended a New York party hosted by fashion designer Fernando Sánchez. When someone asked for help because her friend was being assaulted, Ayer went to see what was happening and found the boxer Mike Tyson pestering a young Naomi Campbell, then at the start of her modeling career. Ayer promptly told Tyson to stop. The boxer turned on him and said, "Do you know who the fuck I am? I'm the heavyweight champion of the world." To which Ayer replied, "And I am the former Wykeham Professor of Logic. We are both pre-eminent in our field; I suggest that we talk about this like rational men." Which is what they did, while Ms. Campbell quietly slipped away.

became Grote Professor of the Philosophy of Mind and Logic at University College, London, a position he held until 1959. He moved to Oxford that year, having been appointed Wykeham Professor of Logic.

During the 1930s Ayer had attended meetings of the Vienna Circle (see box on page 142) and in his first book, *Language, Truth and Logic* (1936), he presents the classic English version of logical positivism. He makes it clear that there are only two types of knowledge: knowledge that is empirically verifiable (it can be tested by observation) and knowledge that is analytic (it is true by definition, according to linguistic rules). Scientific statements and statements of everyday fact are examples of the former, while mathematical statements and statements of logic are examples of the latter. Ayer takes the argument further by saying that, if propositions fall into *neither* camp, they must be devoid of meaning, boiling down to mere expressions of personal opinion. To this category he consigns religious and metaphysical statements such as "God exists"—or "God does not exist"—as well as the idea that there is a realm of things out there, existing beyond phenomena.

In *The Problem of Knowledge* (1956) and also in *The Central Questions of Philosophy* (1973), Ayer reiterates the idea that the role of the philosopher is to use logic to clarify the basic concepts of science, not to come up with schemes—whether based on metaphysics or theology—that provide great insights into how things really are.

Michel Foucault

(1926—84)

"What is philosophy today…if it does not consist
in, instead of legitimizing what we already know,
under-taking to know how and how far it might be
possible to think otherwise?"

—*The Use of Pleasure*

Born and raised in Poitiers, France, Michel Foucault went to
Paris after the Second World War, where he attended the Ecole
Normale Supérieure. In addition to studying philosophy he
developed a great interest in psychology after a period of acute
depression, briefly teaching the subject at Lille University. After
spending some time abroad, he returned to France and started
lecturing in philosophy, first at Clermont-Ferrand and then at
Vincennes, before becoming Professor of the History of Systems
of Thought at the Collège de France in Paris in 1970.

Foucault drew on his interest in history, philosophy, psychology and linguistics to analyze the relationship between history
at large and the history of thought. He did not see how history
could be treated as a unified process capable of revealing objective truths or coming up with universally applicable lessons,
since the knowledge available to people in any given historical
period is bound to be conditioned by existing social norms,
forms of cultural expression, the ways language is used and the
prevailing philosophies of the time: in other words, systems
of thought. Seen in this light, it's clear that what counts as
"normal" for human beings is fluid, determined by different
factors at different times.

HARDWIRED FOR LANGUAGE

MIT Professor Noam Chomsky (1928–) started a revolution in linguistic analysis in his *Syntactic Structures* (1957),

where he challenged the accepted view that children acquire language through instruction and experience. For Chomsky the speed with which it is mastered suggested that there must be an innate predisposition for language within children. He took this to mean that an unlearned, universal grammar exists, supplying rules that can be recognized immediately.

Within his system, there are two levels of linguistic knowledge: deep structures, which refer to the universal grammar shared by all languages, and surface structures, which cover specific words and sounds used in a particular language. To Chomsky's mind we are all born hardwired for language. His *Cartesian Linguistics* (1966) reiterates the rationalist—and therefore anti-empiricist— implications of this idea.

To get at the concepts that underpin these systems of thought, Foucault adopted what he called an "archaeological" approach. Choosing specific historical periods within which to work, he studied often overlooked areas—psychiatry, medicine, punishment systems, sexual behavior—to uncover the conditions that make certain practices, institutions and theories possible.

As far as Foucault was concerned, it all came down to power, which could be looked at through the prism of those whom society chooses to exclude: the insane, prisoners, sexual deviants. In *Madness and Civilization* (1961), he claims that Enlightenment "reason" packaged up madness and consigned it to the asylum, while *The Birth of the Clinic* (1963) treats medical understanding in a similar way. Things billed as progressive and humane advances in treatment were, he says, just aspects of social and political control. By looking at prisons, *Discipline and Punish* (1975) demonstrates how the meaning of punishment can change over time.

Foucault is not saying that power and freedom are incompatible or that power is automatically a bad thing—it's simply a fact of life. But the idea that freedom is something objective that can be protected by the state is a fallacy, as his studies of history make clear. Likewise, the suggestion that truth can be found through the pursuit of rationality is just another historical invention. The search for truth, especially the truth about ourselves, remains valid, but there are no easy answers. The role of philosophy is to help us to think through the hard ones—in other words, the previously unarticulated thoughts.

Jacques Derrida
(1930–2004)

"There is nothing outside of the text."
—Of Grammatology

Born in Algiers, Jacques Derrida studied at the Ecole Normale
Supérieure in Paris and taught there for twenty years, from 1964,
after a stint teaching philosophy at the Sorbonne. Renowned
as the founder of deconstruction, his work was initially seen as
relevant only in the field of literary criticism—where texts can
be studied independently of their authors' intentions—but he
was eager to see his new approach applied to philosophy at large.

Three of his books published in 1967—*Speech and
Phenomena*, *Of Grammatology* and *Writing and Difference*—
introduce and expand the basic concepts of deconstruction,
which center on theories of signification, indication, ideality
and sense or meaning in general. To paraphrase the jargon,
Derrida maintains that earlier philosophical systems have all
been constructed on the basis of conceptual oppositions: for
example, internal vs. external, transcendental vs. empirical,
universal vs. particular. One of these terms is always privileged over the other, which is then excluded. By analyzing
what's been excluded, Derrida shows that the preference for
one term over the other is in fact groundless, because what's
privileged has meaning only by virtue of being contrasted to
what's excluded; it has no meaningful significance otherwise.

There is no grand system for Derrida, no generally applicable
standards of truth in the outside world—critical textual analysis
is all. And in highlighting the limitless possibilities of interpreta-

PRETENTIOUS...*MOI*?

Derrida's approach was not universally welcomed in academic circles. When Cambridge University wanted to award him an honorary degree in 1992, there were protests from a number of leading academics who claimed that Derrida's contributions amounted to "little more than semi-intelligible attacks upon the values of reason, truth, and scholarship." Meanwhile, Chomsky (see page 155) accused him of using "pretentious rhetoric" as a way of masking the simplicity of his ideas, and even Foucault (see page 154) was moved to say that Derrida wrote so obscurely that you couldn't follow what he was saying half the time and that even if you did, but then criticized him, he would accuse you of being too stupid to understand.

Perhaps his critics were too stupid to understand. They were outvoted, and Derrida received his honorary degree.

tion—which effectively means the impossibility of a definitive interpretation—Derrida draws attention to the fact that Western philosophy's attempts to establish certainty through reasoning have always been based on the shaky ground of promoting certain interpretations and suppressing others.

SOME METAS, -ISMS
AND -OLOGIES

Atomism: Things can be understood once they have been broken down through analysis into distinct and independent components.

Conceptualism: Abstract concepts exist, but only in the mind.

Critical realism: There is some ultimate truth, but it is always limited in scope.

Deconstructionism: Analysis of philosophical and literary language through the study of the internal workings of concepts and language—for example, the relations between meaning and the assumptions that lie behind forms of expression.

Deism: Belief in the existence of a supreme being or creator who does not intervene in the universe (see theism).

Deontology: Study of the nature of duty and obligation.

Determinism: All events and actions are ultimately determined by causes external to the will (see libertarianism).

Dialectical materialism: Marxist view that political and historical events result from social conflict as a result of material needs and can be seen as a series of contradictions and their resolutions.

Dualism: Division into two categories or elements (*see* Monism).

Emotivism: Value judgments, especially ethical judgements, express emotions rather than representing facts.

Empiricism: All knowledge is based on experience derived from the senses.

Epistemology: Study of knowledge, particularly its methods, validity and scope—"How do we know what we know?"

Existentialism: Existence of the individual as a free and responsible agent determining his or her own development through acts of will.

Functionalism: Things are no more or less than the functions they fulfill in an overall system.

Humanism: Attaching prime importance to human rather than divine or supernatural matters.

Idealism: Objects of knowledge are dependent on the activity of the mind.

Ideology: System of ideas and ideals; negative connotations in Marxist theory, where dominant ideology is determined by ruling classes.

Libertarianism: Belief in free will rather than determinism (*see* Ideology).

Logical positivism: Form of positivism (see below) that considers the only meaningful philosophical problems those that can be solved by logical analysis.

Materialism: Everything that exists is material or depends on matter for its existence.

Metaphilosophy: Theory about the nature of philosophy.

Metaphysics: Branch of philosophy concerned with first principles of things, including abstract concepts such as being and knowing.

Modernism: Modern ideas or styles that aim to break with traditional forms, particularly associated with the late nineteenth and early twentieth centuries.

Monism: There is only one substance or one world, and reality is one (see dualism).

Naturalism: Nature and the natural sciences lie at the root of all things, so there is no need for supernatural or spiritual explanations.

Nominalism: Universals or abstract concepts are just names, without any corresponding reality.

Ontology: Branch of metaphysics (see above) concerned with the nature of being.

Panentheism: God is greater than the universe, including and merging with it.

Pantheism: God is identified with the universe or the universe is a manifestation of God, making God and nature one.

Perspectivism: Ideas are rooted in particular perspectives, so there are any number of possible schemes for judging truth or value.

Phenomenalism: Human knowledge is confined to the appearances (phenomena) presented to the senses, or appearances are the foundation of knowledge.

Phenomenology: Science of phenomena as distinct from the nature of being; study of consciousness and objects of direct experience.

Positivism: System that recognizes only what can be scientifically verified or is capable of logical or mathematical proof.

Postmodernism: Late-twentieth-century style and concept in the arts, architecture and criticism; represents a departure from modernism and is characterized by the self-conscious use of earlier styles and conventions, a mixing of different artistic styles and media, and a general distrust of theories.

Rationalism: Reason rather than experience is the foundation of certainty in knowledge.

Realism: Universals or abstract concepts have an objective or absolute existence.

Relativism: Knowledge, truth and morality exist in relation to culture, society or historical context and so are not absolute.

Solipsism: The self is all that can be known to exist.

Structuralism: Human cognition, behavior, culture and so on can be analyzed by focusing on the contrasts between inter-related elements in a conceptual system.

Subjectivism: Knowledge is simply subjective, without external or objective truth.

Teleology: The explanation of phenomena by the purpose they serve rather than by postulated causes.

Theism: Belief in the existence of a god or gods, specifically a creator who intervenes in the universe (see deism).

Utilitarianism: Actions are right if they are useful or for the benefit of the majority.

Putting Philosophy
to Work

Answer the following questions in as many ways as you see fit—preferably with friends and a large glass of wine.

◎◎

If I say this sentence is not true, am I telling the truth?

◎◎

If a tree falls in the forest when no one is there, does it make a sound?

◎◎

If all the swans I have ever seen are white, does that mean all swans are white?

◎◎

If a lion could speak, would I understand what it was saying? If my car is only a car because we've all agreed to call it a car and really it's just an intellectual construct, will it still cause a lot of damage if it crashes?

⊚⊚

If my brakes fail as I'm driving toward a group of children crossing the road, am I justified in steering the car up onto the sidewalk and knocking just one pedestrian down?

⊚⊚

If the soles and heels of my shoes are replaced again and again, are my shoes still the same shoes?

⊚⊚

If I have a face transplant, am I still me?

⊚⊚

Can a person travel back in time beyond when they were born? Can a robot be human?

What are your *life questions?*

_____

_____

_____

_____

_____

BIBLIOGRAPHY

Berlin, Isaiah. *The Age of Enlightenment*. New York: Mentor Books, 1956.

Blackburn, Simon (ed.). *Oxford Dictionary of Philosophy*. Oxford: Oxford University Press, 2008.

Boardman, John, Jasper Griffin and Oswyn Murray (eds.). *The Oxford History of the Classical World*. Oxford: Oxford University Press, 1986.

Chambers Biographical Dictionary. Edinburgh: Chambers, 1990.

Chambers Dictionary of World History. Edinburgh: Chambers, 1994.

Critchley, Simon. *Continental Philosophy: A Very Short Introduction*. Oxford and New York: Oxford University Press, 2001.

Critchley, Simon. *The Book of Dead Philosophers*. London: Granta, 2009.

Grayling, A. C. *The Meaning of Things*. London: Weidenfeld & Nicolson, 2001.

Hampshire, Stuart. *The Age of Reason*. New York: Mentor Books, 1956.

Honderich, Ted (ed.). *Oxford Companion to Philosophy*. Oxford: Oxford University Press, 2005.

Kaufmann, Walter (ed.). *Existentialism from Dostoyevsky to Sartre* (extract from Jean-Paul Sartre lecture translated by Philip Mairet). New York: Meridian Books, 1989.

Knowles, Elizabeth (ed.). *Oxford Dictionary of Quotations.* Oxford: Oxford University Press, 2009.

Kohl, Herbert. *The Age of Complexity.* New York: Mentor Books, 1965.

Mautner, Thomas (ed.). *Penguin Dictionary of Philosophy.* London: Penguin Books, 1997.

Monk, Ray, and Frederic Raphael. *The Great Philosophers.* London: Weidenfeld & Nicolson, 2000.

Oxford Dictionary of National Biography. Oxford: Oxford University Press, 2004.

Pirie, Madsen. *101 Great Philosophers.* London and New York,: Continuum, 2009.

Rosenthal, M., and P. Yudin. *A Dictionary of Philosophy* (translated by Richard R. Dixon and Murad Saifulin). Moscow: Progress Publishers, 1967.

Russell, Bertrand. *History of Western Philosophy.* London: George Allen & Unwin Ltd., 1961.

Soanes, Catherine, and Angus Stevenson (eds.). *Oxford English Dictionary.* Oxford: Oxford University Press, 2005.

Urmson, J. O., and Jonathan Rée. *The Concise Encyclopedia of Western Philosophy & Philosophers.* London and New York: Routledge, 1989.

INDEX

ENJOY THESE OTHER
READER'S DIGEST BESTSELLERS

I Used to Know That

Make learning fun again with these lighthearted pages that are packed with important theories, phrases, and those long-forgotten "rules" you once learned in school.

Caroline Taggart
ISBN 978-0-7621-0995-1

I Used to Know That: Geography

It's hard to know everything about the interaction of diverse physical, biological, and cultural features of the Earth's surface. Explore all of it with this entertaining, easy-to-understand little book.

Will Williams
ISBN 978-1-60652-245-5

I Used to Know That: Civil War

Taking you beyond the history book, these pages bring to life colorful personal stories of heroes, brilliant military strategists, blunderers, guerillas, outright villains, spies, secret sympathizers on both sides, and their wives on the home front.

Fred DuBose
ISBN 978-1-60652-244-8

I Used to Know That: Shakespeare

Capturing the unbelievable scope of Shakespeare's influence, this book will surprise and delight you not only with fascinating facts and little-known details of his life but also with the surprising legacy of the language and phrases inherited from his works.

Liz Evers
ISBN 978-1-60652-246-2

i before e (except after c)

Featuring all the memory-jogging tips you'll ever need to know, this fun little book will help you recall hundreds of important facts using simple, easy-to-remember mnemonics from your schooldays.

Judy Parkinson
ISBN 978-0-7621-0917-3

cartes ⊚⊚ John Locke ⊚⊚ Baruch Spinoza ⊚⊚ Gottfried Wilhelm Leib

uel Kant ⊚⊚ Jeremy Bentham ⊚⊚ Georg Wilhelm Friedrich H

rx ⊚⊚ Friedrich Nietzsche ⊚⊚ Bertrand Russell ⊚⊚ G. E. Moore ⊚⊚

ul Sartre ⊚⊚ A. J. Ayer ⊚⊚ Michel Foucault ⊚⊚ Jacques Derrida ⊚⊚

⊚ Parmenides ⊚⊚ Anaxagoras ⊚⊚ Empedocles ⊚⊚ Protagoras ⊚⊚ Socrates ⊚

⊚⊚ St. Augustine of Hippo ⊚⊚ Avicenna ⊚⊚ St. Anselm ⊚⊚ Averroes ⊚⊚

rasmus ⊚⊚ Niccolò Machiavelli ⊚⊚ Thomas Hobbes ⊚⊚ René Desc

erkeley ⊚⊚ Voltaire ⊚⊚ David Hume ⊚⊚ Jean-Jacques Rousseau

penhauer ⊚⊚ John Stuart Mill ⊚⊚ Søren Kierkegaard ⊚⊚ Karl Marx

Wittgenstein ⊚⊚ Gilbert Ryle ⊚⊚ Karl Popper ⊚⊚ Jean-Paul Sartre ⊚

⊚⊚ Pythagoras ⊚⊚ Xenophanes ⊚⊚ Heraclitus ⊚⊚ Parmenides ⊚⊚

Seneca ⊚⊚ Epictetus ⊚⊚ Marcus Aurelius ⊚⊚ Plotinus ⊚⊚ St. Augus

⊚⊚ Thomas Aquinas ⊚⊚ William of Ockham ⊚⊚ Desiderius Erasr

pinoza ⊚⊚ Gottfried Wilhelm Leibniz ⊚⊚ Voltaire ⊚⊚ David Hume ⊚

rt Mill ⊚⊚ Søren Kierkegaard ⊚⊚ Karl Marx ⊚⊚ Friedrich Niet

⊚⊚ Karl Popper ⊚⊚ Jean-Paul Sartre ⊚⊚ A. J. Ayer ⊚⊚ Michel Fouca

naximander ⊚⊚ Anaximenes ⊚⊚ Pythagoras ⊚⊚ Xenophanes ⊚⊚ Hera

Aristotle ⊚⊚ Epicurus ⊚⊚ Seneca ⊚⊚ Epictetus ⊚⊚ Marcus Aurelius

Maimonides ⊚⊚ Roger Bacon ⊚⊚ Thomas Aquinas ⊚⊚ William of O

cartes ⊚⊚ John Locke ⊚⊚ Baruch Spinoza ⊚⊚ Gottfried Wilhelm Leib

uel Kant ⊚⊚ Jeremy Bentham ⊚⊚ Georg Wilhelm Friedrich H

rx ⊚⊚ Friedrich Nietzsche ⊚⊚ Bertrand Russell ⊚⊚ G. E. Moore ⊚⊚

ul Sartre ⊚⊚ A. J. Ayer ⊚⊚ Michel Foucault ⊚⊚ Jacques Derrida ⊚⊚

⊚ A. J. Ayer ⊚⊚ Parmenides ⊚⊚ Anaxagoras ⊚⊚ Empedocles ⊚⊚ Protagoras

⊚⊚ St. Augustine of Hippo ⊚⊚ Avicenna ⊚⊚ St. Anselm ⊚⊚ Averroes ⊚⊚

rasmus ⊚⊚ Niccolò Machiavelli ⊚⊚ Thomas Hobbes ⊚⊚ René Desc

erkeley ⊚⊚ Voltaire ⊚⊚ David Hume ⊚⊚ Jean-Jacques Rousseau

penhauer ⊚⊚ John Stuart Mill ⊚⊚ Søren Kierkegaard ⊚⊚ Karl Marx

Wittgenstein ⊚⊚ Gilbert Ryle ⊚⊚ Karl Popper ⊚⊚ Jean-Paul Sartre ⊚

⊚⊚ Pythagoras ⊚⊚ Xenophanes ⊚⊚ Heraclitus ⊚⊚ Parmenides ⊚⊚

Seneca ⊚⊚ Epictetus ⊚⊚ Marcus Aurelius ⊚⊚ Plotinus ⊚⊚ St. Augus